AF480669

TRUST BUILDERS

Trust Builders

The Key to Thriving Communities

Amy Holloway

Published by Game Changer Publishing

Front Cover Design by Color & Light with Interaktika Studio

Author Photo by Carol Spags Photography

Paperback ISBN: 979-8-90158-117-9

Hardcover ISBN: 979-8-90158-091-2

Digital ISBN: 979-8-90158-092-9

www.GameChangerPublishing.com

This book is my opportunity to celebrate people I have met throughout my career whose gift of building trust has made a lasting impact on their communities. I want to share their stories to inspire others. I sincerely thank the thirty-one Trust Builders who shared their time and brainpower with me.

The book is dedicated to my family and friends, especially to my husband, Chris, who has been my steadfast cheerleader for more than twenty years.

To my parents, who have both passed on. My mom, who shared her brilliant humor and gifted me with confidence to be my creative self. My dad, who insisted that girls could do anything boys could do, and gave me a love of the outdoors. To my sisters, too, for keeping it fun and real.

To my "framily" as well. Dear, encouraging friends like Trent, Joe, Angie, Tommy, Pat, the Steps, the Coxens, Amanda, Naila, Marcos, Ann, Sue, the welcoming and wonderful Asheville crew, and so many others, whose grounding, guitar nights, and silliness keep me afloat.

It takes courage to put your ideas on paper, and I could never have lifted a pen without the support of my friends and family.

READ THIS FIRST

Just to say thanks for buying and reading my book,
I would like to connect with you!
Scan the QR code here.

Here you can share your own Trust Builder story, take the free Trust Builders Strengths assessment, and contact me about speaking at your next event or facilitating a workshop.

TRUST BUILDERS

The Key to Thriving Communities

by Amy Holloway

CONTENTS

PART THREE
YOUR CALL TO ACTION

INTRODUCTION

Why do communities with similar assets experience very different outcomes? Why do some places thrive while others flatline, even if, on paper, they appear to be almost the same?

After thirty years of working with local leaders across America, I've come to believe that trust is the single most powerful force behind economic growth and community prosperity. When local leaders across nonprofit, business, education, and government sectors truly trust one another, when they set aside personal agendas and act with integrity for the good of their community, extraordinary things can happen.

This book is about intracommunity trust: the kind that fuels collaboration, accelerates progress, and has the potential to transform entire regions. It is about trust among organizations that together shape a community's future.

Through interviews with thirty-one remarkable Trust Builders from cities across the country, I've explored what makes certain communities hum with possibility while others stall in division. In this book, you'll read their stories and leadership lessons on creating whole cultures of trust that drive measurable results: robust economic growth, better jobs, healthy local businesses, and a higher quality of life for everyone in a community.

Improving trust and translating it into stronger communities is entirely achievable. By understanding their trust-building strengths and intentionally applying those skills, anyone in a civic role can build relationships that strengthen their local economies.

IS THIS BOOK RIGHT FOR YOU?

To decide if this book is right for you, I'd like you to answer a few questions:

- Think about your volunteer and professional life. Are you any of the following: economic development professional, chamber of commerce member, philanthropist, or other nonprofit executive, employee, or board member; business manager or entrepreneur; government supervisor, staff, or elected official; school administrator, teacher, or PTA parent; developer, landowner, or real estate professional; community volunteer; or otherwise civically active individual?
- Are you someone who cares about the community where you live, and do you have a role in making your neighborhood, city, or even region a better place?
- Does something about what you do have an impact on your community's future?

If you answered yes to any of these questions, this book is for you. You have the potential to become a Trust Builder and deepen the skills you already possess. Every action you take to strengthen relationships with others who serve your community will create far-reaching ripples, shaping a stronger future.

WHY NOW?

I'm writing this book in 2025, when our nation is experiencing profound change. I believe the encouragement this book shares is needed and timely. **This is a reminder that there are very good people doing very good things every day in our local communities.**

In a time when distrust is headline news, this book offers a different narrative. It shares real stories about how trusting relationships inside local communities are driving progress and new opportunities for Americans every day. I hope this helps shift focus away from negative national rhetoric and instead spotlights the uplifting impact of things taking place today at the neighborhood, city, and regional levels. The dedication of local leaders to positive change at home is foundational to our country's future.

COURAGE OVER CAPITAL

Why do communities invest millions of dollars in infrastructure, work-force programs, marketing campaigns, and other initiatives—which are all important—but few intentionally invest in building trust among local leaders? Of the more than two hundred community organizations I've worked with in my career, I've never seen a budget line item for "trust building," even though, as this book argues, it is the single most important factor in developing a thriving economy.

The exciting thing is that trust building is not subject to monetary constraints. It can provide a competitive advantage that is completely within every community's grasp if they are willing to devote time and focus to it. It takes more courage than capital. As we discover in this book, there are day-to-day actions that local leaders can take to strengthen and repair intracommunity trust. In fact, nearly every person has at least one trust-building strength that, when put to work, can build stronger bonds that lead to positive change in their communities.

My purpose is to help you learn from other local leaders in places across America. The Trust Builders I interviewed for this book share tactics for fostering trust that have greatly contributed to their communities' progress. Many of their tips are easy to implement. Trust-building may seem like an amorphous topic, but it is a skill set that anyone can put into action.

BOILING THE OCEAN

This book might inspire further research on this topic. While my premise of trust among local leaders being a top competitive advantage in economic and community development has been supported through my observations and interviews, I recognize that it just scratches the surface. After this book is published, I plan to continue interviewing Trust Builders, hosting conversations, and being on the ground helping clients with strategic planning.

I will also research the broader topic through my Practitioner-in-Residence position at Harvard Kennedy School's Reimagining the Economy project. I thank Rohan Sandhu and the team for giving me the opportunity to explore this topic in more detail. Some initial follow-on ideas are to deepen research, quantify and index trust, create classroom guides and community workshop materials, and consider how this work intersects with management and public policy theory.

I realize that trying to understand the impact of trust on economic and community development could feel like trying to boil the ocean. I'm okay with that. For those who need more detailed evidence before acting, know that it is forthcoming as my research continues. For others, I hope my observations and the leadership lessons from the incredible thirty-one Trust Builders in this book are enough to spark a change in the way you think about strengthening your community.

PART ONE
TRUST IS THE KEY TO THRIVING COMMUNITIES

This book is organized into three parts.

Part 1 sets the scene. Here, I present my premise and evidence to show that trust among community leaders is a powerful asset. It provides insights into why this topic is critically important today, offers examples of trust-building at work, and explores how personality traits lead to different types of action. It also includes questions to help you identify your own trust-building strengths, what I will call "Trust Strengths" in this book.

Part 2 shares condensed transcripts of my one-on-one interviews with thirty-one local leaders across the country. Part 3 highlights findings from the interviews, including the six specific actions that leaders take to build trust, as well as a call to action to help you start a culture of trust where you live.

In the following pages, I start by giving you a foundation for understanding trust and how to use it deliberately as a force for change.

1
THE TRUST ADVANTAGE

"The ability to establish, grow, extend, and restore trust is the key
professional and personal competency of our time."
– Dr. Stephen M.R. Covey

Around fifteen years ago, I was working as a strategist for two mid-sized regions in the U.S. They had each engaged me to help their local leaders—CEOs, elected officials, nonprofit executives, education administrators, and others—come together around a unified plan to improve their region's economy. The two planning processes started around the same time and followed similar tracks. I was committed to making both a success.

Facilitating an economic development strategic plan is like assembling a jigsaw puzzle. A lot of factors must fit together to make an economy vibrant and healthy for the people and businesses located there. Pieces of the puzzle include local industries, workforce, infrastructure, housing, public policies, community image, quality of life, and the list goes on. When factors are misaligned or missing, communities may experience economic decline, job losses, and brain drain. In my role as a consultant, I look for missing puzzle pieces as well as those that connect everything together but need amplification.

I relish the experience of helping places plan their futures. I have built my career around it. I love discovering what makes a place special, and I enjoy hearing from local people about why their community is unique and what they feel could be improved. I even like digging into data to understand how a place stacks up against others. Through qualitative and quantitative research, I find it rewarding to uncover what's working and what isn't.

Through my work with more than two hundred communities over the past thirty years, I have become adept at helping local leaders address problems and build on strengths. Ultimately, my work helps communities grow their economies: create good jobs, start and expand businesses, increase wages, retain people, and gain wealth. I like to say that I am driven to create more prosperous places.

Throughout my career, I've observed that the core puzzle pieces important to economic and community development are often consistent across communities. For example, it helps to have (to name a few):

- A skilled workforce
- Businesses and suppliers across a diversity of industries
- A healthy, safe, and family-friendly lifestyle
- Unique, locally owned shops, restaurants, and cultural amenities
- Land, sites, and utilities that support business growth
- Transportation access, like highways, rail, and efficient air service
- Public policies that encourage business growth
- Relative affordability and access to quality homes, childcare, and transit
- Communications campaigns to reinforce positive messages about the community

However, I have also clearly noticed that places with similar assets don't always have similar results. Two communities could have all the features listed above, plus others, but not achieve the same level of economic growth. How can that be? Why can one place perform so much better than another if they start with the same puzzle pieces?

This question brings me back to the two projects I just referenced. Both clients, at the time, were similarly sized with similar assets. Both had high-level leaders involved with enough resources to get projects done. However, one was beginning to exhibit significantly better economic performance than the other. I asked myself why the contrast was so stark. And then the "Aha!" moment happened.

About halfway through the planning process, several leaders from one of the regions called and requested that more people be involved. They asked me to spend time in one of their underrepresented communities to engage their neighborhood leaders. They felt like the strategy would be more effective if additional people were given a voice.

My team and I traveled there, held meetings in the neighborhood, and invited several of those leaders to serve on the project's steering committee. They ended up playing a crucial role in the outcome of the strategy by pivoting our focus and helping us redefine what success meant for the overall region. It changed the committee's perspective and brought others along in the reasoning. The willing-ness and trust of those leaders to be inclusive of others redefined outcomes and continues to help that region stand out above others today.

The next day, I received a call from several executives in the other region. They said they were becoming uncomfortable with the plan-ning process and wished we weren't casting such a wide net to gather input. Specifically, they asked me to make sure a certain organization would not be included in the process going forward. They "didn't trust them."

The request to leave out a few organizations had more of an impact than just a single meeting. People could sense that there was tension, and divisions started to form. Instead of what was best for the commu-nity as a whole, the focus became on who could benefit the most from the plan.

We were caught in the middle, and the call volume increased with people vying for their individual interests to drive the strategy. While we threaded the needle, creativity and boldness suffered. In the end, the plan we formed was good but not great. Today, that region is performing modestly. I believe they could have attained a higher level of success had it not been for the distrust among local leaders.

AHA!

Following that experience, I began to focus more closely on trust within my client communities. In top-performing communities, I have observed an elevated level of trust among local leaders. They tend to listen to each other, show up reliably, act honestly and authentically, and openly share information. I noticed that strong trust advances a community's starting line, amplifies resources, increases agility, compresses timelines, and provides a higher baseline for seizing transformative projects. Those with high levels of distrust tend to stick with the status quo and even decline over time.

In essence, after thirty years in the field, I believe that trust among local leaders is the greatest differentiator between a prosperous economy and one that doesn't reach its potential. It is the key to a thriving community.

I also believe that there are lessons that everyone can take to help foster trust and make their communities better places. Through interviews with thirty-one Trust Builders across the U.S., this book illuminates those lessons.

SMALL TOWN, BIG TRUST

Since I started focusing on trust-building, I have had the privilege of working with numerous places that validated this premise, including one small town in the American South. During my first visit, I asked the local chamber of commerce to assemble area leaders for a focus group. These folks included the mayor and local business executives, the president of the local college, nonprofit administrators, and others.

To familiarize myself with the community, I kicked off the meeting by asking them to tell me about the strengths of the city. In unison, they chimed in with stories starting as far back as a century ago. There were fist bumps and high fives as they talked.

The legacy of their shared goals, setting sights high and working together, was pervasive in how they related to each other. Like when they recruited their first college…in the 1890s. And then their second college. When they invested in downtown and park improvements. When they expanded their roadways and launched a major marketing campaign. When they supported a nonprofit with securing a game-changing grant and another with a co-working space.

I watched them as they recounted their many points of pride and saw them celebrating, excited to have an opportunity to share stories and emphasize their commitment to carrying forward together.

Later that evening, they invited me to a reception with more than a hundred other community members of all ages and backgrounds. A local band played as they served drinks and food from area businesses. The enjoyment of being together was palpable. They welcomed me openly and continued telling stories. Throughout the rest of my visit and while working with them, I sensed trust and alignment in every meeting I attended.

With a population of 70,000-ish people, this town could have had the same struggles as some other similarly sized places in its state: loss of jobs and businesses, depressed downtowns, and failing companies. However, their local economy consistently and substantially outperforms the state average. According to the U.S. Census Bureau, from 2015 to 2025, this town's population grew nearly 3.5 times faster than the state average (51 percent versus 14 percent).

I am convinced that the camaraderie among their local leaders plays a significant role in their success. Their culture of trust places them on a bigger playing field and allows them to take on projects that might feel too big for other places their size. Since visiting, I have told many others about this town. They unintentionally converted me into a cheerleader for them, the penultimate "flywheel effect," as people in my industry like to say, because I am still bragging about them today.

UNDER SURVEILLANCE

Around ten years into my career, a mid-sized region engaged me to lead their first economic development strategy. Coming into the project, I knew this region had a reputation for divisiveness, but I saw potential and was encouraged that past issues stemmed from a lack of a strategic plan.

When I arrived at the client's office, I noticed something odd. Their lobby was windowless, with a desk, a logo, and a small couch. A closed door led to the rest of their offices. There was no receptionist, but a security camera was mounted in one corner of the room. The physical space said, "We don't trust!" The inside of the office was no better. I counted at least twelve small rooms off a narrow hallway, with most doors closed.

Now, don't get me wrong. I'm not an interior designer, and I certainly understand it when nonprofits lack resources for an expensive office suite. I also appreciate that confidentiality is important. But something about this, the camera and a dozen closed doors, made me feel like I was under surveillance. And then I thought, *if I feel like this... what message is this sending to their community partners and visiting businesses that might want to invest in this region?*

The physical environment was an indicator of the state of the region. During the six-month planning process, there were secret meetings, excluded partners, and even an attempted takeover of the organization by a group of local government leaders.

I called a special meeting of the executive committee to discuss the trust crisis I was observing, one I believed could only be resolved by a change in organizational leadership. In the end, they opted for no change. Their strategic plan, designed to align partners and better connect with their local college, failed to realize its potential. In the ten years that followed, the job growth of its largest neighboring MSA (metropolitan statistical area) was nearly five times faster, and the state's job growth was nearly three times faster.

THE POSTER CAMPAIGN

Early in my career, I had the opportunity to work for a county that was home to a large branch of the state's university system. The campus had interesting R&D and a vibrant student population. Coming from Austin, I'm always energized by university towns and can see their innate economic development potential.

During our first meeting in this community, we heard that the university president and the chamber of commerce CEO were at odds. An argument had taken place. The details aren't important, but the aftermath is. The chamber CEO was actively advocating for the university president to resign. To make her point, the chamber CEO printed flyers stating that the president was "terrible," so to speak, and taped them on walls around campus.

You can imagine what a stir this caused. Trust was in jeopardy. A full-on battle was taking place right as we were starting their strategy. And as you'll hear me repeat, a working strategy depends on trusting relationships among the community leaders. With this complete destruction of trust, their strategy started in deficit mode.

We believed that the university played a critical role in the local economy, but we recognized that the city itself had a problem: its downtown was eroding. Businesses were leaving, restaurants couldn't stay open, and other shops were closing. We also knew that the university was in the process of launching a new graduate school, which would attract even more students to the community.

The university depended on the city to remain vibrant, thereby attracting students and faculty. The chamber needed the university to be strong so that students and faculty could support downtown businesses and generate a lively atmosphere. At the end of the day, they wanted the same thing. They just needed to see their common ground.

During the strategic planning process, we sought to repair the broken trust between the two leaders. Through numerous meetings and negotiations with other community partners, the chamber CEO and the university president called a truce. In turn, the university decided to locate its new graduate program downtown, which revitalized the community and fostered an environment that invigorated students and faculty.

Creating a culture of trust begins with repairing or establishing relationships between individuals within a community, and trust, or lack thereof, can become viral. Renewing trust between two individuals by reminding them of their shared priorities can initiate a healing process that leads to long-term progress. As one Trust Builder interviewee said, "Interpersonal trust begets institutional trust," and that cultivates a culture of trust.

SEEKING RELIEF IN THE COVID-19 AFTERMATH

I would be remiss not to mention the place-based industrial programs launched by the U.S. government between 2022 and 2024 (some of which are ongoing). In response, in part, to the COVID-19 pandemic, the U.S. Department of Commerce's Economic Development Administration (EDA) created several rapid-fire grant opportunities with award sums larger than any I'd seen in my career.

The $1 billion Build Back Better Regional Challenge (BBBRC) program and the $500 million first phase of the Regional Technology and Innovation Hubs (Tech Hubs) program provided U.S. regions with an opportunity to compete for $1.5 billion in funding for potentially transformative investments in community development. Additional funding was available through competitive grants like the 2024 National Science Foundation Regional Innovation Engines program (a potential of up to $1.6 billion for ten awardees over ten years) and the 2022 and 2024 American Rescue Plan's Good Jobs program (up to $525 million distributed amongst 40 regions).

In both the BBBRC and Tech Hubs programs, communities were given a three-month deadline for submitting their first-round grant applications. This accelerated timeline was challenging, considering the dozens of local partners needed to develop a compelling request. Each grant applicant had to identify up to eight transformative community projects for funding, plus have a sign-off from every organization that would play a role. This was equivalent to the federal government creating an Amazing Race for economic developers, and competition was intense.

At the core, these grants were a test of trust. **Those communities whose leaders already had strong trust, shared vision, and experience in working productively together were at an immediate advantage.** Their starting line was far ahead of that of others with weaker relationships. Of the 529 applications submitted, for example, only twenty-one received Build Back Better awards (ranging from $25 million to $100 million each). When I look across those victors (and my team and I worked with one on its application), for many of them, I can see a correlation between the win and the deep local relationships that were formed long before the grant opportunity came about.

I don't know if other opportunities like those will come along in the years ahead. Priorities have changed, but the lessons remain. The sizable dollar amounts incentivized local leaders across America to form coalitions, agree on a vision, and prioritize community projects.

There is debate over whether monetary incentives like BBBRC and tech hubs lead to lasting trust and deeper relationships or if, after the funds dissipate, people go their separate ways again. (The study of the effectiveness of place-based industrial policies like these could be an entire book on its own.)

Based on my observations and optimistic outlook, I would argue that regions that competed but were not awarded grants are now better positioned to collaborate on future projects. The pursuit showed that they could set aside differences and work together toward a common goal. There is a residual benefit to experiencing the process together. For those awardees, the bonds formed during the pursuit process will hopefully be long-lasting, carrying through the trials associated with administering the grant and implementing the funded projects.

Either way, it is certainly a test of trust. The impact will take time to unfold.

MY HOPE FOR THIS BOOK

This is a book to celebrate the good. It is designed to highlight the stories of local leaders who cultivate a culture of trust in their communities and whose actions lead to meaningful, positive change. Through my experience, supported by inspiring interview narratives and other research, I provide specific steps for building trust and fostering stronger communities.

I believe that trust is a critical topic today. Collaboration at the local level can help repair fractures at the state and national levels. The people profiled in this book demonstrate that trust among local leaders is attainable and can be harnessed to foster prosperity within communities.

There are plenty of stories of bad actors and struggling communities. With a quick internet search, I can find tales of what not to do. That is not what this book is about. It is also not about political viewpoints or activism. The Trust Builders and lessons featured on the following pages represent the potential of local communities across America, regardless of party lines. I have witnessed this firsthand for three decades. It starts with a single action and a willingness to connect with other humans.

Positive change starts locally, and local progress requires trust.

2
NAVIGATING THIS BOOK

"For the future of our field, everything starts and ends with trust."
– Nathan Ohle, International Economic Development Council

Many times, conversations among business professionals center on what someone does or how they do it. In economic and community development, conversations might focus on projects that were won or lost, lists of local assets, or descriptions of community issues.

I estimate I have met with more than 20,000 people since beginning my career in 1995. The vast majority of these discussions were fact-finding in nature. Often, my conversations focus on framing a strategic plan. I ask questions to learn more about their community's strengths, challenges, and new opportunities. I seek input on vision, goals, and tactics for the future. Maybe you do the same when you meet with other leaders in your community. Perhaps you are gathering information or trying to reach consensus.

Writing this book was an utter delight. It gave me an opportunity to delve deeply into the character and leadership traits of people I admire. It was a luxury to have time with these leaders, to hear their stories from the field, gain understanding about what makes them tick, and learn about their personalities and how their strengths translate into their approaches. I thank the interviewees with all my heart. These conversations got my synapses firing. I hope they will do the same for you.

Approach

I began by developing a wish list of local leaders with whom I've either worked or I know through my networks. I refer to these individuals as "Trust Builders." I started with more than a hundred people and then narrowed the list to ensure geographic and demographic diversity. As with any selection process, it was not perfect, but it was a start. In fact, I intend for this to be just the beginning of many more interviews in the future. There are far more than thirty-one local Trust Builders in America, including you.

Prior to the interviews, I shared with them the same eight questions:

- On a scale of one to ten, with one being not at all relevant and ten being the most critical factor, to what degree does trust among community leaders contribute to success in community and economic development?
- Based on research and my own observations, I'm exploring eight strengths of Trust Builders. They are (1) active listening, (2) authenticity, (3) competency, (4) empathy, (5) integrity, (6) reliability, (7) respecting differences, and (8) transparency. Which two or three strengths best describe you as a Trust Builder?
- What specific things do you do to build trust with others in your community?
- What are some ways leaders in your community foster trust with each other?
- Please share an example of a time when trust played a significant role in helping your community seize an

opportunity (or avoid a crisis). Was there a time when a lack of trust created a problem or a loss?

- Tell me about a shortcoming you have shared in a way that helped build trust with others.
- Tell me about another community leader whom you deeply trust and why.
- What advice would you share with someone who wants to improve their ability to build trust with others?

During the interviews, I often began with the first two questions and then let the conversation unfold. Some became more story-based, others philosophical, and still others tactical. The interview chapters in Part 2 are condensed transcripts of my conversations, edited for flow. I removed filler words but preserved the voices and personalities of the Trust Builders. These are their actual words. I wanted their personalities to shine through. My voice is interspersed, too. It's written to be immersive and narrative-driven, like listening to a podcast.

When an interviewee raised a unique point, I followed wherever it led. I asked questions with you in mind. I focused on providing practical advice whenever possible, right down to specifics, such as who to engage first when there is a new opportunity or how frequently certain meetings take place. I also asked for details when a Trust Builder's story was about a situation that you also might encounter in your work as a local leader.

You'll see common themes across the interviews, but don't worry; this is not robotic or copy-and-paste. This is not written by artificial intelligence…I need to say that. It is all original content. There was no ghostwriter or team of interns doing this work. It was all led and written by me and founded on my experience. It just happened, to my delight, that the themes I heard were similar whether I was hearing from someone in a rural community or someone in a large metro area.

The interview chapters are grouped by the top Trust Strengths of each leader, in alphabetical order: active listening, authenticity, competence, empathy, integrity, reliability, respect for differences, and transparency.

I want to note that the thirty-one interviewees ended up being almost evenly distributed among the Trust Strengths: three to five for each strength. And all Trust Builders had multiple strengths.

I must give credit to author and social commentator David Brooks. His book, *How to Know a Person,* inspired my mindset as I led the Trust Builder interviews. His insights into seeing another person through a lens of curiosity inspired me to ask questions that delved into the character of each Trust Builder. Additionally, his perspective on connecting with others helped shape the questions I asked. I recommend that anyone in a community leadership role read Brooks' book to help their interactions move beyond surface-level status reports and "how-tos" and to build trust by being immersed in who a person truly is.

HOW TO USE THIS BOOK

Part 1 of this book explores my premise around trust and community development. It also shares findings from my Trust Builder interviews.

Part 2 includes condensed transcripts from the interviews.

Part 3 summarizes the six tactics of Trust Builders and offers a call to action that will help you put this book to work.

It's completely up to you how you approach Part 2. I hope you will cozy up in your favorite chair as you read and feel like you are in the room with them, having a conversation, just like I did.

It might be interesting to read the interviews in Chapters 6 through 36 in order from beginning to end, but you don't need to. You could skip around to interviews with people who share your trust-building strengths or read interviews with people who have strengths that you don't. Perhaps you will read interviews with people who live in your community or in places you enjoy visiting. Or maybe you will read one interview a day and reflect upon it.

Underline ideas, make notes in the margins, and cross through things you don't agree with. Use a highlighter to mark up passages that resonate with you. Tag pages. Start a trust-building "how-to" journal.

That's to say, how you move through Part 2 is completely up to you. Do whatever it takes to make reading it a valuable experience for you.

This book can serve as a learning platform for you, your staff, board members, students, and local partners. For example:

- If you are part of a civic organization, you could ask your colleagues or board members to read this book and use it as the basis of your next meeting or retreat.
- If you are part of a community project, you could invite other team members to explore the trust tactics described in Part 3, and everyone could commit to doing one thing.
- If you work for a nonprofit, government, or socially oriented business, you could ask your colleagues to answer the Trust Strengths questions in Chapter 5 (or take the online version of the assessment) and then review them together during your next staff meeting.
- If you're a teacher, you could assign students passages from this book as a way to teach them the often-unwritten skills needed to make a stronger impact in their future careers.
- Individually, you could read a Trust Builder interview chapter every day for one month and start a journal reflecting on the lessons they share.

You may also conduct your own Trust Builder interviews with your local community partners. Ask the same questions that I used in my interviews and go from there. Discuss lessons learned, stories that resonate, how trust shows up in your own community, and how you will personally commit to improving trust. While I've never worked with an organization that has a budget line item for trust-building, perhaps the time you dedicate to reading this book could be a start.

I would love nothing more than for this book to inspire greater collaboration and relationships in communities across the country.

I believe that greater prosperity in America starts at the community level and emanates upward. It begins with strengthening trust among local leaders.

3

DEFINING TRUST

The Merriam-Webster dictionary defines trust as "assured reliance on the character, ability, strength, or truth of someone or something." ChatGPT says trust is difficult to explain because "it is a concept that is both emotional and rational. It is fundamental to all human relationships and the functioning of society. Trust involves a willingness to be vulnerable to others, despite uncertainty, because one has a positive expectation of their actions." In essence, it is an emotional and complex topic, and its meaning often depends on context.

INTRACOMMUNITY TRUST

There are numerous books on trust within individual relationships, such as with families, spouses, partners, and others. There are also many leadership books aimed at building trust within corporations.

I am not a psychologist or an organizational management expert. But I am a specialist in the topic of economic and community development. I have spent my entire career observing trust within hundreds of communities. In this book, I examine trust at the intracommunity level. This is trust between groups located in the same place, in which people from different organizations or civic volunteer roles collaborate and build relationships to make their neighborhoods, cities, and regions even better places.

With that in mind, in this book, "trust" is understood as occurring when local leaders set aside personal agendas for the good of their communities, consistently and with integrity.

There you have it.

Here, the words "set aside personal agendas for the good of the community" may also be described with terms like "civic responsibility," "collective responsibility," "stewardship," "intrinsic leadership," "civic duty," "community altruism," "public service," and other terms. "Consistently" means just that—leaders frequently prioritize community on a regular versus one-off basis. And "integrity" relates to character—someone who has high moral and ethical values and acts the same way publicly as when no one else is watching.

COMMUNITY DEVELOPMENT VERSUS ECONOMIC DEVELOPMENT

You'll see me intermix the terms "economic development" and "community development." To me, they are essentially the same. An older approach to economic development was to focus almost entirely on attracting new companies into a town. In fact, in the earlier days of the profession, it was referred to as "industrial development," and the organizations responsible for that were often called "industrial development authorities."

Note: Today, these standalone nonprofits are often called "economic development organizations." The function of business attraction might also be found within chambers of commerce and/or local governments. Almost every community in the U.S., regardless of size, has at least one professional dedicated to this role.

As the field has advanced, perspectives have become increasingly holistic. Now, economic development is truly community development. One cannot grow a prosperous economy through business attraction alone. Supporting the growth of existing companies and entrepreneurs is also critical.

All this centers on people, the workforce, and the surrounding support in terms of public policies, schools, infrastructure, research and development, networks, and lively, healthy neighborhoods and downtowns. It's like a jigsaw puzzle, as I mentioned earlier. What pieces don't fit? Which ones are missing?

That is why the Trust Builders I interviewed embodied a diverse range of people in various roles. As I said in the introduction:

- **Trust Builders include anyone whose professional or personal roles impact the future of their community.** This can occur in visible public ways, such as a city mayor, or chamber of commerce president, or school superintendent, and in less visible ways, such as an owner of a local boutique or a volunteer with a local nonprofit.
- Here, **"local community" is open for interpretation. While I am primarily referring to entities with geographic boundaries—a neighborhood, city, county, or multi-county region—there are lessons in this book for anyone seeking stronger trust within their network**. In that case, "local community" could be more broadly defined to include groups with whom someone affiliates (e.g., a school, small business association, arts group, faith-based organization…you get the point).

TRUST BREAKERS

In the spirit of keeping this book positive, I will only mention briefly what Trust Builders *do not do*. Let's call people who do these things "Trust Breakers." Overall, Trust Breakers might insert themselves into a community project (e.g., creating a workforce training program, attracting a new company to town, expanding the local airport, launching a marketing campaign…the list could go on) with the intent of doing something that benefits only themselves or their organizations, even when it sets back (or ruins) collective progress.

Thus, "setting aside personal agendas" is part of the definition of trust. It is critical.

Trust Breakers might exhibit bad behaviors, like in some of the stories that I shared in Chapter 1. These could include:

- Failing to keep commitments
- Pointing fingers at someone else when mistakes happen
- Withholding information or distorting facts
- Gossiping and bad-mouthing others
- Taking credit for others' work
- Excluding people
- Interrupting and talking over people
- Refusing to attend meetings if certain people are invited
- Dismissing others' feelings

Yikes! Have you ever experienced a Trust Breaker or seen this bad behavior get in the way of community progress? I won't delve into Trust Breakers any further. You get the point.

Identifying what not to do, like those things listed above, is a good starting point for anyone who wants to be a Trust Builder. Essentially, "show up with positivity, do what you say you'll do, and stay above the line" could be a useful mantra to begin the path toward becoming a Trust Builder.

4

PUTTING TRUST TO WORK

Based on my experience over the past thirty-plus years as a strategist, I can say without hesitation that trust among local leaders:

- **Shortens timelines.** Places with high levels of trust respond more quickly. When a new community project or opportunity comes their way, they can move nimbly even without complete information. They save time otherwise spent in rounds of discussions about whether to pursue a project, in side-bar meetings, or throwing doubts into the mix as they consider their own personal agendas. As a bonus, the time they save from Trust Breaker activities allows them to devote more time to innovation.
- **Lowers risks.** Have you ever been involved in a community project that got derailed once you were well into the initiative? High trust reduces risk. There's less chance of being caught by a surprise that jeopardizes progress. People show up reliably, follow through on commitments, share information in a timely manner, and bring their "A" game in terms of competence.
- **Amplifies resources.** In trust-based communities, you often find local leaders who share goals and readily pool funds to

pursue a shared vision and priority projects. Trust can turn six small budgets into one impactful initiative.

- **Creates an elevated foundation.** For the three reasons above, a heightened level of trust allows places to take on more transformative and innovative projects. Their baseline for action is higher. Local leaders are more comfortable thinking creatively and pushing limits when they feel supported and unjudged by others in the community.
- **Evolves into a flywheel effect.** Trust among local leaders leads to higher-performing economies. Rinse and repeat. When trust results in successful projects and community wins, it strengthens bonds and makes the leaders involved more confident about working together on future initiatives.

You'll see these benefits echoed throughout the Trust Builder lessons. As you read this chapter, consider the way trust among local leaders has impacted your ability to make progress in your community. Then think about how that trust-based progress has been measurable.

It may be that local leaders united to support the attraction or expansion of a business. The result can be measured in terms of new jobs created, increased productivity, or higher tax revenue. Or it could be that local leaders came together to build a new technical school (measured in higher education levels), a downtown or housing investment (measured in population growth and retail expenditures), or even a public policy shift that encouraged all the above to take place.

TRUST REINFORCES TRUST

Dr. Stephen M.R. Covey, in *The Speed of Trust*, argues that trust is a measurable asset that can deliver quantifiable value. It helps projects happen at a lower cost and higher speed. In his research, the ability to foster trust comes from a person's character and competence. His work echoes what I heard from my interviews with Trust Builders: people have innate trust-building strengths, and they also employ tactics to form closer ties with others. It starts with building trust between two people and then radiates upward to institutions and culture as a whole.

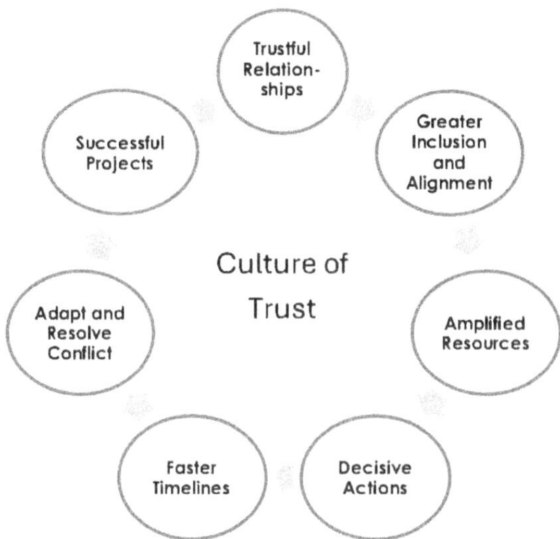

I am especially interested in the flywheel effect of trust. To me, it looks something like this image.

Notice that "Culture of Trust" is at the center of this flywheel. A culture of trust is the expectation that all local leaders agree to set aside personal agendas and work together for the good of the community. When new leaders enter an organization, or when someone is promoted to a leadership role, they adopt the same mindset because that expectation is part of the local culture. Others would view it as bad behavior if they didn't.

When trust relationships exist at the intracommunity level, local leaders feel comfortable including more people in projects. It is assumed that they will act with integrity, too, so there is nothing to fear.

Next, with the alignment of local partners, a community can coalesce resources. They aren't mincing up money to pursue their own agendas. Rather, they combine and find that "one plus one equals three."

With that, local leaders can take more decisive actions, thereby shortening timelines. People are more willing to take risks together, so they spend less time trying to subvert another organization's agenda. They resolve conflicts as they arise without halting progress. This results in projects coming to fruition and reinforcement that trust is paramount to success.

EVOLVING TRUST WITHIN YOUR COMMUNITY

Another theme from my interviews is that creating a culture of trust begins at the individual level. Every place, no matter how divisive, has the potential to evolve into a culture of trust, but it often starts with establishing, repairing, and maintaining trust between two (or maybe more) local leaders.

My earlier example of the poster campaign between the chamber of commerce CEO and the university president is a good case in point here. Because those two individuals mistrusted each other, members within their organizations followed suit. Chamber staff and even some board members complained about the

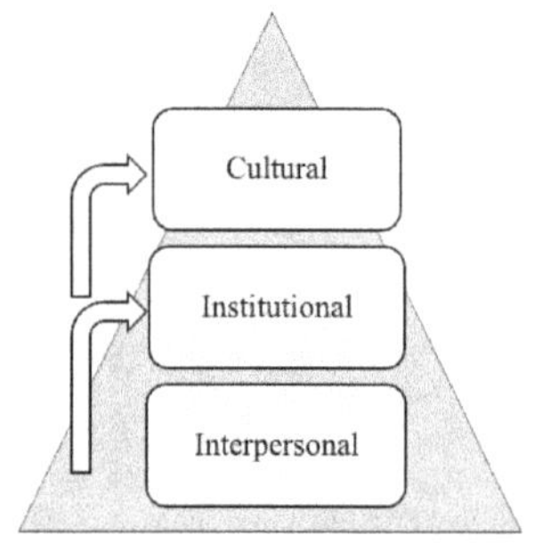

university and stopped attending meetings with certain administrators and faculty. Similarly, university leaders disengaged with the business community and became increasingly insular. All of this fed a culture of mistrust across the community. Other local leaders took sides. You can see how this began to spiral into dysfunction.

Once trust between the chamber CEO and the university president was restored at the interpersonal level, institutional and cultural damage began to heal. Witnessing their organizations' leaders getting along again defrosted tension among their team members. Walls came down, and people started working together again, focusing attention on positive community projects.

Another example I heard is more humorous but nonetheless poignant. One leader I spoke with told a story about how he was perplexed about why no one ever refilled the toilet paper at the park where his son played baseball. When he asked the city administrator about it, she said the park was jointly managed by the school and the city parks department. At one point, the superintendent and city manager got into an argument, and after that, both refused to maintain the park's restrooms. My interviewee then said, "But one of those people retired, and the other one died ten years ago! Why does this continue to be a problem?"

That's a case where interpersonal mistrust led to residual institutional and cultural mistrust. For anyone reading this, the first step toward repairing trust and progress at the intracommunity level might be as simple as restocking toilet paper, or whatever that is, where you live.

Taking that first step to establish or repair interpersonal trust may seem insurmountable at times, but the Trust Builders in this book offer practical guidance. As one said, "I start conversations with 'Can we agree that…?'" What are the shared interests or beliefs in the sliver at the center of the Venn diagram of interpersonal interests? Begin there and then nurture.

Trust might erode if it's unattended. Many of the Trust Builders interviewed offer tactics for nurturing and maintaining a culture of trust once it's achieved, from a regular cadence of meetings and outreach to a free flow of information. You will see plenty of examples in the transcripts in Part 2.

CREATING A SAFE SPACE

Providing a safe space is critical to creating a culture of trust. A safe space is an environment (e.g., a regularly-scheduled meeting in a neutral location) where local leaders can freely confront issues together. Trust Builders create these spaces deliberately, even if it starts reactively. They have thoughtful agendas, time for social connection, and shared learning. They include people in different roles with different points of view. They happen on a routine basis—weekly, monthly, or quarterly, for example.

Safe spaces must be built to last. Without a deliberate commitment to sustain them, there is a risk that they will elapse before real progress takes hold. Trust is fortified when the space is reliable and explicitly enduring: "We're committed to this for as long as it takes." While the space may form in response to a single, pressing community challenge, it can evolve into a forum for tackling future issues as well.

I heard about this from multiple Trust Builders. To design your safe space, first clarify the focus of the work. The issue itself may feel amorphous or too large, so it is important to articulate the issue at hand and break it down into components. Second, identify and understand the perspectives of the factions affected by the challenge, and map who the allies and contrarians might be. Know who your local partners should be. Third, ensure those meetings are safe by using structured agendas, listening sessions, and acknowledgment of frustrations.

TRUST BUILDER TACTICS

In *Bowling Alone*, Dr. Robert D. Putnam, political scientist and professor emeritus at Harvard Kennedy School, describes trust as a component of social capital that is essential to the possibility of cooperative action. He describes "generalized reciprocity" (doing things for others without expecting anything specific in return, knowing that others will help if needed) as key to transforming cultures and communities over time.

I value Dr. Putnam's work because he examines the practicalities of trust at the intracommunity level, including broader perspectives on civic engagement. In his research, activities like volunteering, voting, participating in public meetings, and being involved in schools and faith organizations can lead to a "sociological superglue": bonds and bridges that help communities achieve greater outcomes. These are tactics that many people in your community, regardless of position, can use to contribute to a more trusting culture—volunteer, vote, or donate, for example.

For local leaders like you, actions can be even more deliberate. In my interviews, I asked Trust Builders about their real-world experiences. I then distilled those findings into tactics that you can employ as well. They range from consistently showing up and following through on your promises to finding common ground, giving others the spotlight, and being a mentor. In Part 3, you'll find a concise playbook drawn from those conversations to help you take the next steps in building trust within your own community.

5

STRENGTHS OF TRUST BUILDERS

Let's personalize this even more. My interviews revealed that all Trust Builders share at least one of the following strengths. These strengths, either intrinsic to the individual or earned through practice, help them build bridges and engage with other leaders in their communities. They include:

- **Active listening:** Being wholly present in conversations with others, absorbing themselves in what other people are communicating, rather than thinking ahead about what they will say next.
- **Authenticity:** Being completely themselves, whether they are at work or at home, letting their true personality shine, and being honest with others about their beliefs.
- **Competency:** Having knowledge and specialization and sharing those insights with others in the community to inform and advance progress.
- **Empathy:** Deeply understanding others, sensing their emotions, and feeling compassion.
- **Integrity:** Doing the right thing even when it might not result in a win for them or their organization in the short term.

- **Reliability:** Consistently showing up when they say they will and following through on their commitments.
- **Respecting differences:** Actively seeking out people whose views are unlike their own and being genuinely curious about others' viewpoints.
- **Transparency:** Proactively sharing information and being upfront with others about their intentions.

Stated another way, it would be difficult for someone to be a Trust Builder without having at least one of those eight characteristics. And, as reiterated in my Trust Builder interviews, anyone who is civically engaged will benefit their cause and community by enhancing these skills.

You likely already have a few of these strengths. However, you may never have considered your talents through a trust-building lens. You may be interested in strengthening your capabilities as a Trust Builder to accelerate progress in your own community.

When reading this chapter, you might think about areas for self-improvement. Perhaps you are reliable and highly competent, but you struggle to be yourself around others or to be in the moment when listening to someone else. Or maybe you consider yourself to have a high level of integrity, but you don't always invite differing viewpoints.

Wherever you are on the list, think about the following ways to put your Trust Strengths into action:

- **Think about how your top strengths play out in your community.** What specifically do you do to share those skills with other local leaders? For example, if your top strength is transparency, you might be the one who systemically shares data or is willing to share tough news with others. If your strength is active listening, you may have a regular cadence of meetings with other local leaders to hear what is on their minds.

- **Think about the strengths you wish you had.** What can you do to improve upon those skills? Remember, practice makes perfect. For example, if you wish you could be a more reliable leader, start with a one-month goal of never missing a meeting that you said "yes" to (and never accepting a meeting invitation that you don't intend to attend). What about your team members and fellow local leaders? How can you help them build skills that complement yours?

You'll learn lessons on these two topics, turning your strengths into tactical action and improving your skills, when you read the thirty-one Trust Builder interviews. On multiple occasions during my conversations with them, interviewees shared detailed examples of how they build trust (and you'll see their strengths evident in those examples). They also discussed their challenges.

As you think about the Trust Strengths, it could also be helpful to reflect on local leaders within your own community. Are there certain traits that are abundant where you live? Are any missing? For example, local leaders reliably attend meetings, but when push comes to shove, they tend to prioritize their own needs over the community's. Or local leaders are highly competent and experienced individuals, but they don't seem to listen to one another.

Recognizing these strengths and challenges at the intracommunity level could lead to deeper work together. You now know that those eight strengths are critical to creating a lasting culture of trust and that such a culture is essential to a thriving community. This book can help you and others (staff, board members, project partners, for example) explore Trust Strengths together. Individually answer the questions below or take the online Trust Strengths assessment (available at www.TrustBuildersBook.com), and come together to compare your top strengths. Ask yourselves, *what can we do together to fill in gaps and better leverage our collective skills?* Then read the Part 2 interview chapters for inspiration and ideas.

DISCOVERING YOUR TRUST STRENGTHS

As you read the following pages, respond to each statement to identify your Trust Strengths. Use a pen or pencil to check the boxes or even make notes in the boxes. Be honest with yourself.

If your reaction to a statement is that it describes you nearly one hundred percent of the time, then answer "yes!" If you exhibit the behavior occasionally, depending on the situation, answer "sometimes." If the statement rarely or never describes you, then answer "not me."

And please don't criticize yourself for the "not me" answers. The goal here isn't to score all "yes!" There should be a balanced number of answers in each column. You wouldn't be a Trust Builder if you weren't open about your areas for improvement.

ACTIVE LISTENING

"On the first Friday of every month, we hosted the mayor, city manager, county commission chair, county manager, superintendent, visitor's bureau, downtown alliance, airport, and others in our conference room. We had an egg timer, and each person gave a three-minute update. We created a safe haven where people with differences could connect."

– Harvey Schmitt, Greater Raleigh Chamber of Commerce

Active listening signals that you value the other person. Trust grows because you give people your full attention.

If active listening is one of your Trust Strengths, then you thrive when others need to feel genuinely heard. Reflect on how you identify with the following statements:

	Yes!	Sometimes	Not Me
When I'm with someone, I focus my full attention on what they're saying rather than planning what I will say next.			
After someone speaks, I can accurately reflect what they said as well as the meaning and feeling behind what they said.			
After conversations with me, people walk away feeling heard and valued.			
I am good at asking thoughtful questions, and I can forget myself as I listen to the person's answers.			

Findings from Trust Builder Interviews

Trust Builders with active listening as a top strength tend to:

- **Regularly convene local leaders.** They want to hear from others. And when these meetings take place, they dedicate time to listening to every attendee. One Trust Builder said that he schedules twenty minutes at the start of each board meeting so that every board member can share an update.
- **Strategically consider how to listen to others based on who they are and the matter at hand.** For example, one Trust Builder, who listed active listening as a strength, said she engages a broad range of local leaders whenever a significant community project emerges. She first determines the order in which each stakeholder should be engaged—first round, second round, etc. She also adapts each meeting agenda to the individual. Having a meeting infrastructure in place helps her focus on what is being said rather than thinking ahead about the next topic that might need to be covered.
- **Be keen observers of unspoken dynamics as well.** While listening, they also watch the other person to pick up on context that they may not be saying out loud. They respond to the physical reactions of a person—whether they lean in, or

cross their arms, or seem impatient—and take that in to better connect.

- **Be visibly in the moment when one spends time with them.** They set aside their smartphones, lean in, and make eye contact as someone speaks. They often play back what they heard to articulate not only the words but also the meaning they picked up.
- **Also have empathy and respect differences as strengths.** They not only actively listen to others, but they do so empathetically to the point that they feel a deeper connection with the other person. Because listening is a strength and something they enjoy, they may be more apt to reach out to disparate voices in the community, including people who might challenge the status quo.
- **Encourage their team members to be out in the community.** Even when their own organizations are not in a lead role on a project, they will send a colleague to attend meetings to hear what others are saying and show their support by listening.

AUTHENTICITY

"Like, if you see me out and about, I'm usually in my favorite trail running shoes and my best Grateful Dead t-shirt. I'm happy about that."

– Ed Gardner, Entergy Mississippi

"My wife and I started inviting people into our home. If we're planning a dinner with leaders around town or staff, we bring them to our house for a picnic. It helps everyone let their guard down. They can see how I live and my teenagers in their full glory."

– Randy Thelen, The Right Place, Inc.

Authenticity signals that you are consistent between your actions, values, and words. Trust grows because people know that the personality they see is the same one in action when they aren't present.

If your Trust Strength is authenticity, you thrive when being real is more appreciated than perfection and polish. Reflect on how you identify with the following statements:

	Yes!	Sometimes	Not me
I show up the same way no matter where I am, with friends and family, community partners, and at work.			
Others in my community describe me as true to myself, straightforward, and genuine.			
My choices align with my values, even when they come with risk. I'm willing to make the harder choice if the decision feels right for me as I am.			
I'm open about my imperfections, and that vulnerability inspires other people to be real, too.			

Findings from Trust Builder Interviews

Trust Builders with authenticity as a top Trust Strength tend to:

- **Openly acknowledge their areas for improvement.** In my interviews with Trust Builders, they tended to balance their strengths with statements about what they struggle with. For example, one said that reliability was one of his strengths, even when he didn't feel entirely competent in certain community development topics. He admitted that he wasn't an expert, and his willingness to be open about that reflected his genuine self.
- **Believe in being honest no matter what.** In various ways, they said, "I admit that I don't have all of the answers, but I always try to do the right thing." Perhaps being honest and vulnerable are characteristics of authentic leaders.
- **Strive to be the same person "on and off the playing field."** For example, one said that he loves to travel in his free time. He brings that spirit to his work by frequently leaving his office to meet people in their communities. People he works with know he is adventuresome, so they don't expect his work

life to involve sitting behind his desk all day. Another said that her background is in science and that her style of asking many questions reflects a scientific process. She reminds people of that so that they know she's not being critical, just curious.

- **Open up their homes.** For instance, one interviewee said, "I've also hosted officials at my house. They can see, well, this is where I live and how I live, and these are my teenage kids. Seeing the real me helps break down barriers and weave relationships."
- **Also enjoy sharing the authentic personalities of the communities they represent.** They acknowledge their communities' quirks, struggles, and strengths. They let the true character of their places shine through. Often, they use humor to paint a picture of their towns, even if it exposes some flaws. After all, no place is perfect.

COMPETENCY

"There is no replacement for doing the work. When you're in the trenches together, side by side, that builds trust faster than anything. Show up, work hard, be competent."

– Brandon Dennison, Coalfield Development Corporation

Competency signals that you are knowledgeable and know how to put your insights to work for your community. Trust grows because people feel confident that you are credible.

If your Trust Strength is competency, you thrive when aptitude and expertise are important to success. Reflect on how you identify with the following statements:

	Yes!	Sometimes	Not me
Others in my community consistently ask me for guidance or advice.			
I intentionally develop my know-how and build experience so that I can stay sharp and helpful.			
When I don't have an answer, I am honest about it and take steps to learn.			
I have the capability to see a community project through to fruition because I have the skills to do so.			

Findings from Trust Builder Interviews

Trust Builders with competency as a top strength tend to:

- **Have technical or tactical backgrounds.** One leader, for example, served as the research director of their organization before stepping into the CEO role. People in the region already respected him as a go-to expert on the local economy. When he took the reins of his organization, he did so with a high degree of credibility. Another Trust Builder led a national anti-smoking campaign when he was a teenager. The trust-building tactics he learned at that early age inform his approach today as the president of a large regional partnership.
- **See that competency is a strong starting point for establishing oneself as a trusted local leader.** This is where many younger professionals start their journey as Trust Builders. If they do their homework, are willing to learn, and act reliably, their network grows, and they have more opportunities to practice other trust-building skills. Competency appears to be one of the first steps.
- **Foster trust with other local leaders more quickly.** This is especially true when they start a new position or move to a new community. Others recognize their knowledge and experience and are more open to engaging with them because their insights and skills can contribute to progress.

- **Encourage their team members to establish their own strong competencies.** They might invest in professional development classes or research subscriptions. Several Trust Builders talked about how they coach their staff members on ways to let their personalities shine when they make presentations. As highly competent people, they recognize that trust is amplified when people can layer authenticity on top of know-how.
- **Are more likely to remark on the role that systems and structures play in fostering trust among local leaders.** I heard comments, for instance, that the structures of city governments or permitting processes can make or break trust. As highly competent people, they were able to identify shortcomings and had tactical ideas for fixing issues.

EMPATHY

"It might sound weird to say that empathy is important to community development. It's critical to connecting with people and building relationships, and that is key to what economic developers do."

– Adam Knapp, Leaders for a Better Louisiana

Empathy signals to others that you care about them and their perspectives. Trust grows when people feel more connected to you because you strive to understand them as human beings.

If your Trust Strength is empathy, you thrive when people feel emotionally safe and connected with you and each other. Reflect on how you identify with the following statements:

	Yes!	Sometimes	Not me
When someone is expressing their feelings, I adapt my tone and pace to express my compassion.			
Others in my community often come to me because I help them feel supported and heard.			
Before offering my input, I take time to understand others' feelings and the meaning behind what they are saying.			
I listen with my heart.			

Findings from Trust Builder Interviews

Trust Builders with empathy as a top strength tend to:

- **Seek common ground.** Because they are so perceptive, these Trust Builders can intuit where people's shared values and needs intersect. As one Trust Builder shared, "To bring people together, I might say, 'I sense we all feel like [XYZ] isn't working right now, but that is very important to each of us. Can we start there?'"
- **Care even more deeply about their communities.** They form close bonds with other local leaders and feel so strongly about them as people that they will go to incredible lengths to support them. They believe that human relationships are more important than projects and will forego any opportunity that might put those in jeopardy.
- **May personalize another person's perspectives, experiencing their emotions.** Internalizing those feelings might compel them to take on more complex challenges and commit to completing them even when others give up.
- **Observe a difference between transactional and relational communities.** Essentially, transactional communities make progress through rapid exchanges. These places are highly efficient and, in some ways, easier for newcomers to plug into. Relational communities are built around connections, shared

identity, and history. It might take longer to form bonds, but those bonds are stickier. Leaders with empathy as a Trust Strength thrive in relational communities.

- **Might also have authenticity as a strength.** As one Trust Builder said about his personality, "I was raised in a family of good storytellers, and I foster relationships by sharing stories." Hearing other people's backgrounds and beliefs helps him be more empathetic and real with others, and thus "more committed to consistently showing up" for them.
- **Believe that empathy grows when people are in the trenches together.** One Trust Builder remarked that there is no better way to get to know someone and understand where they are coming from than to do hard work together.
- **Admit that empathy is a more difficult characteristic to develop if one doesn't inherently have it.** Earlier in the book, I discussed how Trust Strengths can improve over time. That said, it is possible to attain empathy, especially if one strengthens one's active listening skills. To quote one interviewee, "People have a strong capacity to fake empathy, but it's difficult to fake active listening."

INTEGRITY

"Reputations take a long time to establish, and they can be destroyed in minutes."

– Cathy Chambers, Economic Development Professional

"You must be willing to say, 'I know you're looking at this purchase. I don't advise you to buy it, and here's why.' Even if it costs me money at the moment. If I wanted to sell it without any thought of responsibility for what happens, my integrity would be at risk, and I would break trust. That's a big price to pay in the long run."

– Chris Fraser, Avison Young

Integrity is one of the cornerstones of being a trusted local leader. Integrity signals to others that your actions align with your values. Trust grows because people know you won't trade long-term community impact for short-term, personal gain.

If your Trust Strength is integrity, you'll thrive when others need an ethical leader committed to long-term impact over short-term gain. Reflect on how you identify with the following statements:

	Yes!	Sometimes	Not me
Others in my community trust that I will make the ethical choice, even when no one is watching.			
When I make a mistake, I take responsibility. I am accountable for both my positive actions and my missteps.			
I make decisions based on what's right, even when it might be inconvenient or come at a personal cost.			
I give others the spotlight and celebrate their success.			

Findings from Trust Builder Interviews

Trust Builders with integrity as a top strength tend to:

- **Model long-game thinking.** If acting with integrity is a part of the local culture, leaders can stay focused on the future horizon. Even without a detailed plan in place, they can move forward fluidly because they know that other leaders operate with integrity and won't derail progress toward a vision.
- **Prioritize community over self.** This shows up in various ways. For some Trust Builders, this is about giving others recognition for a win, even when they may not have worked as hard to secure it. As one Trust Builder said, "At the end of the day, people know that my team is hard at work, even if we don't get the recognition. Not being in the spotlight maintains trust." Another echoed this when he said, "As long as we

celebrate our success internally, we don't have to be seen externally. My team knows it was our win because we adhered to our values."

- **Believe it is critical to know what their values are and back that up with action.** As one reflected, "Your words and actions should be the same, and you should surround yourself with people who are part of that ethos."
- **Build teams that also operate with integrity**. They invest in professional development and mentor their team members (and others in their communities). Even in the hiring process, Trust Builders seek out people with high levels of integrity. They know that they cannot be in every meeting every day, so the people representing them must act with integrity and have genuine respect for others.
- **See that integrity is foundational for trust building**. Without question, every Trust Builder I interviewed has integrity, even if they didn't cite it as one of their strengths. For this book, I sought to call out integrity as a Trust Strength so that I could focus more closely on the topic. However, trust and integrity are inseparable.

RELIABILITY

"I just say, 'We'll keep coming back. I know you don't feel good about this right now, and that's okay. I'm not going to try to convince you of anything. But I promise we will just continue to show up, and hopefully, at some point, our actions will speak much louder than words.' For me, part of trust building is that: showing up and doing what I say I will do."

— Tania Menesse, Cleveland Neighborhood Progress

Reliability signals to others that you will do what you say you will do. You follow through on your word. Trust grows because you are dependable even under pressure.

If your Trust Strength is reliability, you thrive when others need a consistent, steady leader who shows up time and time again. Reflect on how you identify with the following statements:

	Yes!	Sometimes	Not me
When I promise I'll do something, others can depend on me without sending me reminders. They know they can count on me.			
Others describe me as responsible and consistent. They can relax knowing that I will follow through.			
In high-pressure situations, I am a stabilizing presence.			
I attend every meeting related to a project or opportunity.			

Findings from Trust Builder Interviews

Trust Builders with reliability as a strength tend to:

- **Show up when they say they will.** Trust Builders who are highly reliable are visibly present. Even when they aren't in the driver's seat, they make their support known by participating in gatherings. "Showing up consistently is key," said one Trust Builder. "If you're not present, you're not thought of."
- **Schedule one-on-one meetings with other local leaders as soon as they land in a new role or community.** In one case, a Trust Builder set a goal of meeting with a hundred people during his first ninety days. Another met with 425 board members and investors in his first year on the job.
- **Establish a cadence of activities so that their calendars can be firm well in advance.** Like active listeners, they might host a monthly meeting with other local leaders. That regularity allows them to schedule other obligations around that day and time.

- **Feel comfortable saying "no," and know when to delegate.** Trust Builders do not say "yes" to every offer they receive. Being a reliable person requires careful consideration of one's capacity and committing only to tasks one can fully fulfill. "I don't do anything halfway," said one interviewee. "If I say I'll do it, I fully will. But I don't say 'yes' to many things." Another said they practice thoughtful delegation: "I always try to be there for the mission-critical work."
- **Recognize that the work itself helps foster trust.** Late nights at the office, eating pizza, and working together to meet a deadline might be the best trust-building moment of the year. As one interviewee said, "The work of the work is what builds trust."
- **Have a stabilizing influence when placed in stressful situations.** For example, if an opportunity has a tight timeframe, the Trust Builder might do things like set the calendar of project meetings, determine who will be there and what the agendas will be, and dedicate their time and attention to meeting deadlines. When they show up, they are level-headed and task-oriented.

RESPECTING DIFFERENCES

"If you are uneasy about having a certain conversation, ask yourself why. It is likely that others feel the same way. Pretending everything is fine and moving forward might produce a result that isn't worth the time spent. Stop to assess; do the exploration work. Engage a diversity of perspectives in those uneasy conversations."

– Stephen Causby, Park Pride

Respecting differences signals to others that you are collaborative and curious. Trust grows because you open the table to other viewpoints and you are thorough in considering ideas that might challenge the status quo.

If your Trust Strength is respecting differences, you thrive in inclusive environments in which a program or project can be shaped by a variety of voices. Reflect on how you identify with the following statements:

	Yes!	Sometimes	Not me
People feel safe expressing their full selves around me.			
When I hear an opinion that differs from mine, I respond with genuine interest rather than judgment.			
I proactively seek input from a broad range of people with diverse perspectives, and I give them equal time to share their views during meetings.			
I accept that disagreement happens, but I don't tolerate disrespect.			

Findings from Trust Builder Interviews

Trust Builders with respecting differences as a strength tend to:

- **Give others the spotlight.** Interviewees talked about treating people the way they want to be treated, including letting them be center stage. In meetings, these Trust Builders try to give everyone an equal chance to talk, balancing the room as much as they can to quell the loudest voices.
- **Find ways their lived experiences connect with others', even when they come from different backgrounds.** One Trust Builder I interviewed worked with a European toy company seeking its first U.S. manufacturing location. Their products were designed to be inclusive of children with diverse abilities. Because her personal experience includes working with youth with special needs, she was able to connect deeply with the company, which contributed to its decision to locate in her community.

- **Form friendships with people who aren't exactly like them.**
  They understand that cultivating strong relationships with a
  broad range of people, particularly those who could be
  affected by a community project, is essential to effecting
  meaningful change in a community.
- **Proactively reach out to and include viewpoints that are
  unlike their own.** For Trust Builders with this strength,
  respecting differences is not just a nod to someone who is
  different. They believe that communities can function at
  entirely new levels if they willingly engage people with
  different ideas. More ideas fuel new, innovative approaches to
  community challenges. The keyword here for them is
  "proactive."
- **Are out in the community.** Several Trust Builders with this
  strength are working in places where trust has been broken.
  As one interviewee said, leadership is "literally showing up"
  and meeting people where they are. She said that progress can
  take more time because they are starting from a different place,
  and that builds trust by being there time and time again to
  listen.

TRANSPARENCY

*"Trust is something you build over time. Being an objective voice, providing
truth by way of data, is incredibly helpful. Sometimes, the news isn't good,
but folks know that you'll deliver the truth, and that builds trust."*

— John Hull, Roanoke Regional Partnership

**Transparency signals to others that you are honest. Trust grows
because others know you communicate with candor, your motives
are clear, and you don't obscure information even when it may be
difficult to hear.**

If your Trust Strength is transparency, you thrive in situations when
openly sharing information is encouraged and valued. You might

consider yourself to be an excellent communicator. Ask yourself the following questions:

	Yes!	Sometimes	Not me
If I have data or intel that can benefit my community, I openly share it with others.			
I am willing to step out of my comfort zone to communicate difficult information.			
Others in my community see me as someone who is clear about my intentions. They do not have to guess what my motives are.			
When I have information to share, I communicate it in a way that is easy to understand and accessible.			

Findings from Trust Builder Interviews

Trust Builders with transparency as a strength tend to:

- **See misinformation and lack of information as serious trust breakers.** Trust Builders with this strength, proactively share information. As one said, "Have a regular timing for correspondence with stakeholders. Like, if a building is going to be demolished, make sure the neighbors aren't surprised when they see the bulldozer."
- **Consider their audiences and tailor the format and frequency of communications to suit.** The format for communications might consider how the information is conveyed, e.g., in a newsletter, online, in a one-on-one conversation, or at community forums. The format may also consider who conveys the information. One Trust Builder recognized that he wasn't the ideal spokesperson to build trust with a particular audience, so he engaged another team member to serve the lead role because she had more in common with them.
- **Value honesty.** Even when information is uncomfortable to share, like bad news, for example, these people don't shy away

from candid conversations. They also communicate promptly because they believe that clarity helps progress move forward, strengthening trust. As one Trust Builder said, "I have honest conversations with people about what I'm hearing, good or bad."

- **May also have authenticity and active listening as strengths.** For two interviewees, being themselves means talking with others about their backgrounds and flaws. "Speaking openly about those realities helps build trust," one said. These transparent leaders tend to ask others for ideas and candid feedback. They may travel to meet with another person to show them that their input is valued.

REFLECTING ON YOUR TRUST STRENGTHS

Review your answers to the questions above and add up your "yes!", "sometimes", and "not me" answers. Of the eight, which two or three have the most yeses? These are your top strengths. Which ones have the most checks under "not me"? Those could be areas for improvement.

While this isn't designed to be a scientific survey or a psychological evaluation, it could help you begin to think about your skills. Keep those in mind as you read the Trust Builder interviews in Part 2. Pay attention to those Trust Builders who have similar and dissimilar Trust Strengths. How do they approach building relationships and leading community projects? What can you learn from them? What stories inspire you?

To access this Trust Strengths assessment online, visit www.TrustBuildersBook.com or scan the QR code:

It is free to take and open to everyone. You may also contact us to schedule a Trust Strengths workshop in your community where we explore the strengths of you and your team in more detail.

DISCUSSION GUIDE

If you would like to reflect on your Trust Strengths in more detail, here are a few questions to begin with. If you're reading this book alongside your team members and other local leaders, you could use these questions to guide your discussion:

- What is my top Trust Strength?
- What behaviors or habits of mine signal to others that this is my strength?
- How could I use this strength right now to foster trust among our community's leaders?
- What about my Trust Strengths surprised me the most?
- How can I improve my skills? What steps could I take?
- When I think about my team, what strengths do we have as a whole? What could we look like in action if we combined forces to improve trust across our community?

PART TWO
TRUST BUILDER
INTERVIEWS

"The best way to find out if you can trust somebody is to trust them."
– Ernest Hemingway

The next thirty-one chapters each contain condensed transcripts of my interviews with Trust Builders. The chapters begin with the interviewee's title and biography, followed by their top two or three Trust Strengths. After that, it includes my questions (in bold) and their thoughtful answers.

For reference, here is the order of interview chapters:

6

CHRISTY GILLENWATER

President and CEO, Greater Oklahoma City Chamber

Oklahoma City, Oklahoma

Trust Strengths

Active listening, Authenticity, Empathy

"The expectation here is that you just can't buy your way in. You have to prove that you'll put personal agendas or your own organization's agenda aside for what's best for the community."

Christy is the president and CEO of the Greater Oklahoma City Chamber of Commerce. She previously served as president & CEO of the Chattanooga Chamber of Commerce, and prior to that, president & CEO of the Southwest Indiana Chamber and president & CEO of the Greater Bloomington Chamber of Commerce in Indiana.

In 2012, Christy was named a Certified Chamber Executive (CCE), the only national certification for chamber professionals. Christy led two chambers—the Southwest Indiana Chamber and the Greater Bloomington Chamber—to win the National Chamber of the Year by the Association of Chamber of Commerce Executives (ACCE), as well as the Indiana Chamber of the Year by the Indiana Chamber Executives Association. In 2017, the Indiana Chamber Executives Association recognized her as Executive of the Year. She is the recipient of ACCE's Chairman's Award. Christy was born and raised in Cincinnati, Ohio. She received a Bachelor of Science degree in public affairs from Indiana University and a Master of Business Administration from Ball State University.

Christy, I'd like to hear your thoughts on the notion that trust is one of the most critical factors in community development. On a scale of one to ten, how does it rank?

It's a nine or ten. Whether it's a ten depends on how you unravel it. In my opinion, to have a dynamic, engaged, forward-leaning community, you must have multiple organizations involved. And that will not happen if there is no trust between the leaders of those organizations.

Take any community. There will always be three to six entities, or somewhere around that, that partner and drive things. If there isn't solid trust, it minimizes opportunity.

It's interesting that you quantified the number of organizations at the core of progress. Does that mean that major initiatives typically start with three to six partners and then others follow? And do you think those are the same organizations in different regions?

Yes, the concentric circles surface after the three to six start the motion forward. Whether it's the same everywhere, that depends. For example, the dynamics between local city and county governments, and which ones are most functional. I've been in communities where one of the partners is a philanthropic foundation. In some places, people think of the foundation as the go-to partner before they think of the chamber or economic development group. If it's a university town, the university is one of those critical players. In Oklahoma City, our NBA organization, the Thunder, is one of those core entities. So, it's a little nuanced in terms of the community. But typically, anywhere I've been, it's three to six organizations that lead the win.

I've experienced that. To kick off a strategy, we will begin by identifying those core organizations and understanding the dynamics between them. Then involvement radiates out into, as I've heard you say, concentric circles of leaders. Is that good advice for readers? If you want to tackle a new opportunity, identify that handful of organizations to form the core, and then work outward?

Yes, that's right.

There are times when it's important to involve a large range of people and perspectives. When there are multiple concentric circles. How do you approach that?

Very intentionally. For example, right now, we're working on a large public project. The first idea was to create a task force, but then I realized that even a task force of people is not going to be as effective as going to people one at a time. We need to strengthen the clarity around where everyone is before we call everyone. We also have to consider the infrastructure of meetings. Do we need a formal agenda, or do we want to say, "Here's the topic; let's make this free-flowing"?

How do you determine the best infrastructure for meetings for a big project like that?

It depends on what you want to accomplish in each meeting. For example, if our goal is agreement on a $2 billion bond, the structure of meetings would be different than a meeting that's focused on touching base and maintaining relationships.

It's like Oklahoma City's MAPS program. The structure has been the recipe of our success and is based on the dynamics of our community. The mayor often leads on the vision, and then the city has a thoughtful process to determine which projects are included. Then it is tested and validated. We call on the public to help. We hear their thinking, which influences the amount of money going into various projects and how we talk about them. If 80 percent of people are happy with it, then we hit go. We don't slow the momentum by trying to satisfy the other 20 percent who might not ever agree.

Let's talk about you. You've said that when you came into Greater Oklahoma City, the community already had a solid foundation of trust. Was that a consideration when you took the role of chamber president and CEO?

Absolutely. I had the privilege of working at the Chattanooga Chamber, where I was happy. There were only a few places I would even consider moving to. And Oklahoma City was one. Having been a distant observer for a while, I thought, *These are the people I want to work for and learn from.* Top CEOs, stewards of the community for the last forty years at least. It was clear to me that OKC leaders were very intentional and focused on being servant leaders. There's an expectation that when someone comes into the sandbox, they must play nice and approach things as a servant leader.

As an outsider looking in, did you intuit that culture existed in OKC? Culture isn't exactly written down anywhere or stated in a job description.

It's not, but you can feel that's the intention. It's the way leaders introduce newcomers into the community. It's the structure of the meetings with local leaders, the regularity of meetings between the chamber team, the city government, and others. For example, there's a cadence of meetings that occur every other month. And there are great processes and infrastructure of meetings that people adhere to. I felt that during the interview process, seeing how they were all interacting with each other, even joking with each other. Like it's in the water because of decades and decades of work together. The emerging group of leaders inherits that culture and carries it forward.

What if someone wants to be a part of the leadership circle but doesn't embrace that culture? What if they are a major investor in a chamber, for example?

Sure, there are folks like that in every place. The expectation is that you just can't buy your way in. You have to prove that you'll put personal agendas or your own organization's agenda behind what's best for the community.

When people like that emerge, there's an intentionality around how to involve them. If there is a trust problem, it doesn't mean that the person can't be involved. You engage them when it's advantageous and use the right tools.

This gets us into specifics, Christy, about your trust-building strengths. I've listed eight Trust Strengths. Which ones are distinctly Christy?

I've been pondering those the last few days. I feel like active listening and empathy are strengths.

I also think seeing the talents of those around you and recognizing what they bring to the collaboration is a strength. I love honoring that and articulating to them, "You're so good at X. It's important that you share that, and we will put you in a position to do that."

As you're looking at this pool of leaders, you're assessing this person as very good. Maybe they're very competent in a specific field, or they're reliable, or they're inclusive, for example. And you realize, *Hey! This is a moment where we really need an inclusive person.* You're considering all these factors when you're thinking about how to get someone involved, so it builds on their strengths.

Can you share an example of a win for Greater OKC where trust played a major factor and the right talents were in the right seats?

There are multiple examples, but I think of LA28 and OKC serving as venues for the upcoming Olympics. The mayor had been working on this, building on thirty years of effort, intentional investment by the community, and people having a shared vision. He saw an opportunity for our city to host at least one Olympic sport. He cultivated relationships with two Los Angeles mayors and other LA leaders over seven years. When the opportunity progressed to the point that he realized the next steps would take place in a public setting, he needed an entity outside of city government to negotiate and bring this to our community. So, he tapped the chamber to lead because he trusted us.

I had only been here six months, so he didn't know me that well at the time. But he trusted our entity. He trusted the leaders who selected me.

He trusted the team around me and our volunteer leadership structure. The trust expands beyond individuals because of the way the structure, or culture, has been built intentionally for years.

Is it fair to say that the speed of trust you gained as a new chamber leader in a new community was due to the trust the organization had established with others over decades?

Absolutely. Yes.

There's an expectation that you won't break that trust.

Right. No pressure!

7

CLARK DUNCAN

Executive Director, Economic Development Coalition for Asheville-Buncombe County

Asheville, North Carolina

Trust Strengths

Active listening, Reliability

"Trust makes it possible to quickly leverage relationships and be highly functional in times when there isn't a second to waste. It helps us start closer to the finish line."

Clark serves as senior vice president for economic development and executive director of the Economic Development Coalition for Asheville-Buncombe County at the Asheville Area Chamber of Commerce. He and his team lead industry expansion, business recruitment, equitable workforce development, economic research, and entrepreneurial growth through Venture Asheville.

Over his seventeen-year career in local economic development, Clark has supported the expansion or recruitment of more than sixty employers, resulting in six thousand new jobs and over $2 billion in new investment in Asheville and Buncombe County, including major corporate commitments from Pratt & Whitney, GE Aerospace, and New Belgium Brewing. He has also led the creation of transformative initiatives such as Venture Asheville, Riverbird Research, the Sustainable Manufacturing Council, and Accelerate Buncombe, an accelerated apprenticeship model broadening economic participation. Most recently, he guided the development of the AVL 5x5 Strategic Plan for Economic Recovery, strengthening economic resilience in Western North Carolina following Hurricane Helene.

Clark, let's start with a question I'm asking every Trust Builder in this book: How important is trust in economic development? Can you rank it on a scale of one to ten?

It's a nine or ten. As someone whose whole career is in the public-private space, and the pendulum has swung, as different policy topics have moved through the community, trust is something we spend a lot of time thinking about. The effort of keeping disparate groups of thought together in an opinionated community begins with trust.

And Amy, because you live here, you know Asheville's unique challenges. If I had four hundred acres and thirty developers that were ready to build my next industrial park, maybe there would be a different path forward. But when you have obstacles in the way, like our mountain topography, for instance, your pathway to success looks different. You need a tight team to walk the road, and it's narrower than in other places. And that's okay because I wouldn't aspire to be a community that has a thousand acres of industrial sites but zero quality of life.

I have an open-book approach, and it can get complicated. We have leaders who are left, right, and center. Building bridges is something we are intentional about. Trust is essential to keeping those relationships strong.

How do you strike a balance when you have such diverse opinions?

Part of it is some strategic work we've done in recent years. For instance, making our board more representative of our community and of our strategy. I don't just mean that in age, sex, and race, although I do mean that, but also in other ways. Like, for thirty years, we had no entrepreneurs on our board. And even when we launched the programs of Venture Asheville, there was a disconnect. At the time, we had no champions on the board. We tried to make sure we had representative voices, so we added board members who were business founders.

We also spend fifteen to twenty minutes in every board meeting going around the room and hearing updates from everyone. It builds trust to show each person that they have a valued voice and they are on equal footing with other leaders on the board who might be seen as being higher up the chain.

The structure is purposeful. The more voices are heard, the better our product is. For example, our current chair, Sabrina Rockoff, has implemented more out-of-the-boardroom interactions. Victoria Isley, the president and CEO of Explore Asheville, has an open house at her home with her family. I've also hosted officials at my house. They can see, well, this is where I live and how I live, these are my teenage kids. Seeing the real me helps break down barriers and weave relationships. Even if we aren't best friends with everyone, we need positive relationships for this whole thing to work.

I like the topic of purpose-driven economic development, which I've heard you talk about. How do you instill that higher-level viewpoint in others in the community?

Well, first, you'll see purpose-forward language in our strategies, like the one you just finished for us. We've also concertedly tried to get more people to fully understand what we do and why we do it. It helps to have a board chair and other leaders whose hometown is Asheville. They feel deeply about the community's future and the impact we make.

We've already talked through some specific trust-building tactics, but I want to focus on your personal strengths for a minute. Of the eight Trust Strengths I shared, which ones stand out as being especially Clark-like?

I'm glad I spent some time with this before speaking with you because I wanted to also think through where there's daylight between these traits. I landed on two. One is active listening. There's a huge amount of respect that comes from people who listen first, digest, and talk second. Strategically, if you're trying to build consensus, active listening gives you a chance to drive a relationship. It's about showing respect and diminishing ego. At the end of the day, it helps us build something together.

For the same reason, I leaned into reliability. Showing up with consistency shows respect before you even start to build a foundational relationship. It's not just about face time. It's about demonstrating over and over again that the other person is important to you.

I sometimes run into this with executives in our field. They intend to show up, but their schedules just won't allow it. So, they delegate. Any thoughts on that? There are pluses and minuses to doing so.

Six or so years ago, we realized we needed to be involved in workforce development. For us, this meant working with more grassroots and not-for-profit organizations. That involved taking the chamber into rooms that we'd never been in before. I knew I needed to delegate that role, so I hired great people to do that work. That team spent two or three years just showing up consistently to workforce development meetings and events. We also showed our commitment through our budgets and payroll.

Delegating to the right people and embedding the workforce as a chamber priority built trust with organizations that had previously been disconnected. Eventually, we formed interpersonal trust, which fed institutional trust. You won't have the latter without the former, and that begins with lots of showing up. The personal relationships can be very satisfying, but it can't just stop there. Larger institutional relationships can continue to function beyond my tenure and your tenure, and that is what helps economies thrive long term.

I want to hear more tactical ideas on forging strong relationships.

Healthy relationships between people and organizations don't just happen by accident. Whether it's time in a board meeting, a board social, or a community cookout, we have a structure. We vary our formats, too. Recently, in lieu of a formal board meeting, we hosted a broader leadership meeting, which brought together the chamber board, the EDC board, and all our investors for a community conversation to talk about larger issues that impact economic development. There was a formal agenda and specialists there to lead the dialogue.

Can you share an example of what not to do? A time when a lack of trust created a significant problem.

At one point, we had a big kerfuffle. An inexperienced local elected official inserted themselves into an opportunity we were working on to recruit a new business to town, and that person called the CEO directly. The project exploded in the press and broke trust among the partners.

We also had a time a while ago when local players in our region who weren't familiar with our organization manipulated relationships when they needed policy support. Like, they threatened to pull our funding if we weren't vocally in favor of their cause.

If it makes you feel better, a lot of communities have faced some version of those stories.

Yes, I'm glad that's in our past. At that time, there was a lack of transparency and trust. It was an extremely transactional environment. Then, new leadership stepped in with the belief that trust was about transparency and that we needed each other to be successful. They focused on healing the community and rebuilding trust.

Clark, recently, the world went through the COVID pandemic. Then Hurricane Helene hit Western North Carolina. Two extremely disruptive events in a row. Before we conclude, can you share how trust among local partners helped our region's resilience?

I can't imagine what it would have been like to go through those times without strong communication and solid relationships. The trust among our leaders helped us pull through.

Think about the hurricane-related crisis communications. That required instantaneous trust. Like, I need fifty names that can tell me X, Y, and Z, and we have press conferences at 11 a.m. and 4 p.m. every single day with spokespeople from six unrelated organizations. A foundation of trust makes it possible to quickly leverage relationships and be highly functional in times when there isn't a second to waste. We started closer to the finish line.

Living here through the storm and aftermath, I saw local leaders setting aside the hierarchy, ego, and titles, allowing the nimbleness you're describing. It continues to be remarkable to see!

My final question is, what advice would you offer others who want to improve their trust-building abilities?

I think they could watch someone like Buncombe County's current assistant manager, who emulates trust-building. He is cool-headed, unflappable, and not easily distracted. I appreciate his integrity and generosity. He comes at problems with professionalism and such calmness and confidence. Maybe that's a preference I have in my interpersonal relationships, but his style has built institutional—and ultimately cultural—trust. My advice to others is to emulate these qualities. Also, be accountable, show up, and do what you say you're going to do.

8
AUNDRA WALLACE

President, JAXUSA Partnership

Jacksonville, Florida

Trust Strengths

Active listening, Authenticity

"At the end of the day, you do business with people you trust. If the trust isn't there, the project is not going to move forward."

Aundra Wallace serves as the president of JAXUSA Partnership, the economic development division of the JAX Chamber, leading business recruitment and expansion efforts across the seven counties that make up the Jacksonville region. Under his leadership, JAXUSA announced more than a hundred projects that generated over 15,000 direct jobs and $5.5 billion in capital investment for Northeast Florida from 2019 to 2024.

Widely recognized for his strategic vision, collaborative approach, and proven ability to drive impactful results for the communities he serves, Wallace plays a pivotal role in shaping Jacksonville's economic future and advancing growth throughout Northeast Florida.

Hi, Aundra! I've been hearing a lot of good news about the Jacksonville region lately. I'm curious to hear more about it.

Thanks. We've been saying yes to things that we think we can close and quickly saying no to things that are going to lead us along long runways that may never get off the ground. We're focusing our efforts around talent pipeline development to make sure that our companies have the workers they need. And we're leading with that message. Talent development is our first goal, and business development is our second.

Thank you for agreeing to help me with this project. Early in my writing process, several publishers said that trust isn't a marketable topic right now. I decided to pursue it anyway.

We're in an environment that is all about trust. I don't think that anyone trusts anyone 100 percent anymore. And that's a detriment to society as a whole. So, when you started talking about Trust Builders, I was like, *Yeah, we really do need to get back to that.*

I'm happy to hear that you agree. It's a topic that has been on my mind for many years.

One of my first questions is to gauge how important trust is in economic development. Is it a major success factor, or is it the icing on the cake?

I think trust is the number one factor. At the end of the day, you do business with people that you trust. If the trust isn't there, it's not going to move forward.

I want to hear more about the things that you do to build trust with others in the Jacksonville region. We can think about it in two ways. Trust with other community leaders and then trust within your own team and the companies that you're working with. What are your strengths in these areas?

One of the eight traits you ask about is being yourself. Act honestly and be authentic. When I'm authentic, people know that I'm coming into the conversation as Aundra, and I'm consistent in my viewpoints.

Active listening is a skill that I've used forever. It's part of being authentic, and for me, that means I'm always willing to listen. Hearing people out allows me to provide good feedback and be able to discuss differences. That's because they know that's who I am. That has served me well in negotiations and building teams.

I retooled JAXUSA when I got here. You can't do that without being yourself or without listening. You need to be able to address the differences in the world itself. Like, in other places where I've worked, the initial conversations were often about funding, funding, funding. I had to hear that and have an honest conversation about what the organization was doing with the money that they were already getting. Were they maximizing it? Listening and understanding that if they shifted resources from here to there, they could achieve what they wanted without chasing more resources. Or going outside of their core mission. Those are tough conversations to have, but it's what I've been able to do.

When you come in as a new leader in an organization, what do you do to quickly build trust?

I do it in a way that is non-threatening and gives people an opportunity to get on board. There might be existing leaders on the team with whom I can immediately build trust. Then I train them for what's to come. That's what will carry the organization forward. It makes it possible to retool and make us better going forward. It starts with trust.

I know that you're very strategic. As a new leader on a team like JAXUSA, you came into a culture that had been in place for a long time.

It wasn't easy. I could have made changes in year one, but I couldn't make the wholesale change immediately. I knew when I came in I needed to focus on the region's talent pipeline in year one. So, I got that going in 2020 and carried it through to 2023, when the full organizational retooling effort started.

So, you laid the groundwork for change for the first three years and then started making bigger changes? I'm reading this to mean there was some staff turnover as a result.

Yes. This change is taking place, and you're either part of it or you're not. You need to tell me if you're going to be a part of it, and I'm going to hold you accountable for it. In response, an exodus of some senior staff took place. But we were prepared for the exodus because, for the prior three years, we hired younger, really bright people to fill junior positions, and they were ready to move up.

That requires longer-range vision on your part. As you were making those changes, how did you preserve trust with your investors and others in the community?

I started putting the new people out in the community before change even took place. People started seeing them and thinking, *I know who these individuals are.* They were already interfacing with investors, so when they were promoted, they were already familiar faces. No one questioned their abilities.

That leads into my next question. Did you give those younger team members advice on how to build relationships and trust with local leaders?

I boost their confidence and say, "You're going to lead that meeting without me. And I know you can do it because you're already preparing the information for me. Now it's your turn to present it. But make sure your style is germane to you. Don't try to present as Aundra would. I need you to be you. It should be your storytelling based on your experiences and through your lens." Being out in front of people and showing their knowledge helps build trust with others.

Shifting gears, can you think of a time when trust played a role in a major win for the region?

Yes, it happened early in my tenure. We had a Fortune 500 company that acquired another large, global company. The company needed a new office building and wanted to build its own, but it couldn't come to terms with the city. They started actively pursuing leaving and going to another state. When the mayor found out about it, he had a heart-to-heart conversation with the CEO and came out of that trying to put the blame on me.

So, I hosted a come-to-Jesus conversation. I was honest with the mayor about where the city went wrong, and I shared advice on ways to improve. It was that defining moment that changed the trajectory and course of my leadership. The mayor decided that my team and I were going to run point on the project, and the city would support whatever decisions we made.

After that, trust was restored. I negotiated the purchase agreement of the property and the city's commitment to site improvements, state and local incentives, FDOT road widening, and others. We got the new office tower off the ground, and that built trust with the company's CEO. We were transparent and honest and did what we said we were going to do. That trust has carried over into today.

One would think that following through, doing what you say you will do, would be a given, but it sounds like it's not always the case. Can you share a specific tip on how to ensure that follow-through happens?

I had a Gantt chart from my old project management days, and we used that to detail every step of the process, starting with the end date and working backward. Now my team makes a Gantt chart for every project with every detail. It's down to the week. And when we have our team meetings every Monday, we have what we call a "situation report," which is, what took place last week? What didn't occur that needs to occur this week? We're that detailed on every project.

That builds credibility, too. You can bring a project, no matter how complex, to you and your team, and people know that, and you're going to deliver.

Do you have any advice on what to do when someone's credibility is attacked? I'm thinking of the negative banter on social media, for example, and the NIMBYism out there.

Understand that the press is not your friend. Understand that from the very beginning. I don't care what anybody says—everything is always on the record. Period. There's nothing off the record. If you don't want to have the conversation, you don't have the conversation. When we do interviews, we're putting the facts out there.

Also, understand that your reputation is your income. Protect it at all costs. And unless the person is working for you, you hire them, and you're paying them, no one has your best interest in mind, no matter what the story is. Because they are going to give it their spin 100 percent of the time.

Finally, Aundra, you lead a seven-county region with a diversity of counties: urban, rural, coastal, and such. Do you have any advice on how a regional organization can strengthen trust with local partners?

I let them know I'm here to help them. I personally show up at their local meetings. I'll talk to their county commissioners when politics come up. I am a sounding board when they ask, "How would you say this if you were me?" I help them with their pitch decks.

If they see me as a resource and someone who doesn't take the credit, the trust level goes through the roof. We can be authentic with each other now, and we can admit when we fumble the ball. They are open if I tell them they need to change their approach based on what the data says about the market. Trust levels are better than ever, and we don't take that for granted.

9
DANIELLE CASEY

President and CEO, Las Vegas Global Economic Alliance

Las Vegas, Nevada

Trust Strengths

Active listening, Transparency

"Figure out what makes people tick. But at the same time, don't compromise your mission and your ethics. That's hard to do, but in most cases, if you look hard enough, you can find some sliver. I've found that if you're honest and consistent, you work to earn that trust even if the other person never fully extends it to you."

Danielle Casey is the president and CEO of the Las Vegas Global Economic Alliance, leading regional efforts to strengthen and diversify Southern Nevada's economy. She brings more than two decades of experience in economic development, public administration, and organizational transformation. Previously, she served as president and CEO of the Albuquerque Regional Economic Alliance, where she delivered a comprehensive regional strategic plan and transitioned the organization into a mission-driven public-private partnership. Her leadership background also includes serving as executive vice president of the Greater Sacramento Economic Council and as economic development director for the city of Scottsdale, where her team supported projects that generated billions in economic impact and thousands of new jobs.

Danielle holds a bachelor's degree from Arizona State University and a master's degree in public administration from Northern Arizona University and has been both a Certified Economic Developer (CEcD) and an Economic Development Finance Professional (EDFP) since 2009.

At the time I interviewed Danielle, she was president of the Albuquerque Regional Economic Alliance (AREA). Since then, she moved into the role of president and CEO at the Las Vegas Global Economic Alliance (LVGEA) and the chair of the International Economic Development Council (IEDA) (2026 term).

Danielle, to start, thank you for interviewing with me. I admire you and have followed your career like a fangirl.

This is flattering and awesome. It means a lot to me.

I shared some questions in advance, but they are just for guidance. Let's start with your thoughts on trust among local leaders and the role it plays in an economy.

I was a military kid, so I moved around a lot. I think it makes you a little more observational, with more self-awareness. For example, you go into a new community as an eleven-year-old, and all the kids have Southern accents, but you don't. You have to learn to be more respectful and understand how things are, as opposed to coming in and saying that you already know everything.

Back to trust: People trust you if they see that you're valuing them and what they say, versus steamrolling.

That gets into my second question: What are your strengths as a Trust Builder?

I think you need to get into a community and understand what is important to them and what the culture is like, then adapt. It doesn't mean that you're disingenuous.

When I started my role at AREA in Albuquerque, I was so excited. We did a strategic plan, and it was well received. As part of that, we started a fundraising campaign. One of our big leaders is an impressive female executive, very accomplished. I came to her with my pitch and presentation, and it went well. But then a week went by, and she didn't sign the pledge form. I started to worry, so I called one of her team members. I said, "I thought the presentation went great but wondered why she wouldn't sign."

Her team member said, "She wants you to give her more time. Have coffee, look each other in the eye, and have the conversation in private once or twice." So, I scheduled a coffee meeting with her, and she signed the form without me asking.

That was a lesson in the local culture in New Mexico. It's relationship-based. People expect a level of respect because their families have been here for generations and generations. That runs deep there. So, I realized it would take longer here to build relationships than I might be used to in more transactional markets. But they are going to be stronger in the long run.

You're touching on something that's interesting to me: the difference between building trust in a relational community versus in one that is more transactional. Can you elaborate?

It goes back to understanding the history of every community you're in. I worked in Phoenix and have roots there. Most of the population is not from there. There is a major population influx. It's very open and accepting, along with a can-do attitude. It's growing very quickly, and you have no choice but to react to that growth. I found it to be a little more transactional from that standpoint.

In New Mexico, you might be working with someone's family member, and legislators are floating a bill that could help or hurt individual family members. There are many generations with deep pride, knowledge, and love for the community. That changes their motivations and timeline. They think, *Will this deal be good for my family three generations from now?*

You've worked in strong regions with very different cultures. What have you learned along the way?

One of the big things I've learned, and I tell my younger teams, is that you're very bright and knowledgeable, but you get these things by intuition over time. When you think it's about you, it's rarely about you.

When someone is acting in a certain way, you might think, *They must be upset with me. What did I do wrong?* Most often, it's got nothing to do with you, and you would never guess. It's about getting their kids to school. Or some other conflict that they're dealing with. Things like that. But I think a lot of people have a tendency, we all do, to internalize. I always sit back and think, *I'm going to lean on the assumption it's not about me, until I find out and confirm that it's really about me.*

Sometimes, there is such a great flow of projects happening that you only have time to react. Not worry about how someone feels about you. You need to get everyone together to make it happen and then move. Complex motivations don't have time to ink their way in.

I came into this book assuming that trust is an important factor in growing an economy. I want to hear your thoughts. On a scale of one to ten, how would you rank it?

It depends. It might be a seven if you don't have competition. It's closer to ten if you have to compete. That requires people on both sides of the aisle to get together. In those cases, trust is absolutely critical.

You've talked about the way that structures can either reinforce a stronger culture of trust or open the door for distrust. I've heard something similar from other interviewees. What happens when you have a single individual in a leadership position who totally opposes growth?

Around twelve years ago, I was the new economic development director in a city, and one of the city council members hated economic development. But he was also the number one sandwich eater. If you had a ribbon cutting, he was the first in line for the free food.

Sandwich eater! Hilarious.

So, the first time I met with him, he looked at me and asked, "Well, what do you want? As far as I'm concerned, I would eliminate your entire department. There's nothing you will ever do that will impress or satisfy me."

I said, "I respect that. But it's my hope that I will prove to you that there is a connection between the work we're going to do and your ideals for the community."

He was all about tourism. So, I ran an impact study on the visitors that private businesses brought to the community every month so that he could say that he helped tourism. After that, he was much more supportive.

Figure out what makes people tick. But at the same time, you can't compromise your mission and your ethics. That's difficult to do, but in most cases, if you look hard enough, you can find some sliver of shared interest. I could have been a little indignant about him. But I found that if you're honest and consistent, you work to earn that trust even if the other person never fully extends it to you. But you'll get to a place of understanding and get support when it counts.

Danielle, before you go back to your busy day, is there anything else you would like to share?

I've been thinking about your list of trust strengths, especially transparency. My first local community was the city of Maricopa, Arizona. I was the assistant city manager responsible for economic development. When I was hired, we went from a city of 1,500 people to 5,000 people in eighteen months. By the time I left eight years later, it was 45,000, and four years later, it was 90,000. Very fast-growing.

They just hired a new city manager, and we were working out of an old ADOT trailer; it's like two double-wides stuck together. And we're all working twelve-hour days. I was brand new to the field and didn't have a clue what I was doing. So, the new city manager came in from Texas with a big Texas belt buckle, and he sat back and said, "We have a problem here. This team has zero trust." He made us go through a study on the speed of trust.

Right. Stephen Covey's *Speed of Trust*.

That's right. He made us all read it as an exercise. And you look around the room, and there were people who would never embrace it. But there were other people for whom the exercises did a lot. I think there's something to be said about having your executive leadership team go through exercises like that, especially if it's a new team with a lot of transition. Going through a book doesn't fix everything, but it gives you tools and topics to talk about to address the situation in a more productive manner.

10

ETHAN BROWN

Executive Director, Sonoma County Economic Development

Santa Rosa, California

Trust Strengths

Authenticity, Transparency

"After the 2017 fires, there was a shared sense of responsibility. I knew I had to build trust by putting all my cards on the table. I didn't care who received credit, but this work needed to get done. Not a single one of us could do it alone. That effort helped pave the way for the collaborative work our organizations are now doing and made that collaboration more reflexive instead of avoided due to difficulty and mistrust."

Ethan Brown is the executive director of the Sonoma County Economic Development Collaborative (EDC). During his decade-plus tenure at the EDC, Ethan has also served as the director of business development and innovation, business and expansion program manager, and entrepreneurial services program manager. In those roles, he connected local businesses of all sizes and stages with resources to help them navigate regulatory frameworks, expand their markets, access capital, and find talented employees.

In addition, Ethan has extensive experience working with businesses to prepare for, respond to, and recover from multiple natural disasters and the coronavirus pandemic. Prior to joining the Economic Development Collaborative, Ethan was a principal at a local general contracting firm that he helped launch and grow into a successful business.

Ethan graduated from Sonoma State University with a Bachelor of Arts in Political Science and Government. Outside of his professional role, he enjoys traveling with his wife and can still be found swinging a hammer when the occasional home improvement project pops up.

Ethan, first, thank you for interviewing with me. I was working with you on a strategic plan during the Tubbs fires, one of the hardest times Sonoma County has faced, and I saw you building trust in that time of crisis. How does trust-building play into how you lead every day?

It is absolutely essential to building partnership, where partnership itself is essential to creating the scale needed to tackle significant and persistent challenges. Simply put, if I can't place my trust in a colleague, leader, organization, or initiative, the potential risks to me, my organization, or the public outweigh the benefits. So, how this plays out for me is to always lead by building that trust, however appropriate. Much of this is simply being a genuine person, acknowledging areas for improvement, clarifying the role I am seeking in a partner, and being honest about my abilities.

Can you talk about the Tubbs Fires and how you used your gift of trust-building to pull leaders together? For example, housing availability was already a concern, and then the fires damaged more than 6,000 structures. It intensified an already fraught topic.

After the 2017 fires, there was a shared sense of responsibility for rapid response to the needs of local employers. This included, for the most part, continuity of operations and resources for employees who were immersed in recovering their lives and sense of being.

Up until that point, many local groups and governments were not accustomed to the type of collaboration we see now. You could say it was more of a competitive environment driven by resource constraints. I knew I had to build trust by putting all my cards on the table; I didn't care who received credit, but this work needed to get done, and I knew that not a single one of us could do it alone.

That effort helped pave the way for the collaborative work our organizations are now doing and made that collaboration more reflexive instead of something routinely avoided due to difficulty and mistrust.

How did that trustful culture parlay into other opportunities after the fires?

While I was not the only member of my organization to work on it, the realization of that is probably something I am most proud of. In the aftermath of the 2017 fires, it was blatantly clear that we would not have the local workforce required to recover the lost housing, let alone keep up with demand in an already constrained environment.

In this case, because of the clear need and (at the time) unprecedented nature of the disaster, money wasn't the biggest hurdle; it was finding skilled people to rebuild. The Santa Rosa Junior College turned out to be a wonderful and willing partner to create that workforce. We, and many other local partners, supported them through value engineering and ultimately a federal grant application to fund that programming. Ultimately, we were awarded a $7 million grant from the U.S. Department of Commerce EDA to open our first-of-a-kind Construction and Building Trades Employment Training Center, which opened in September 2024 to a strong reception by the community.

It's truly a case study of turning a crisis into an opportunity. Wow. Okay, let's talk more about your strengths as a leader. I shared eight Trust Strengths of Trust Builders. Any thoughts?

I am authentically, but not offensively, honest. I feel like the present time, more than ever, has been kind to leaders who are not afraid to share their feelings or information that may have been viewed as risky previously. When collaborating with employers and business owners, I am honest about the environment in which I work; government comes with both constraints and benefits. I cannot build trust while hiding or sugar-coating some of the challenges I will face in reaching specified objectives.

That's not easy for most people, as you know. However, I feel that leaders must pair this approach with a positive and realistic outlook on what is possible. If you can establish a pattern of navigating obstacles and achieving results, you will engender a solid foundation of trust among your peers and community leaders.

Finally, what do you most admire in other Trust Builders you know?

Being oneself, committed, competent, and an excellent communicator. Someone who asks, "How can I be a resource?" and sets ego aside to help. I'm thinking of one of my mentors, who is always willing to jump in and sincerely listens to others, often putting himself into the shoes of others. In my opinion, it's important to mix your genuine self into your work with others while still being clear about your role.

11
MEERA RAJA

Senior Vice President, Deep Tech, P33

Chicago, Illinois

Trust Strengths

Authenticity, Transparency

"Making big community projects work requires many entities coming together. The main goal among all those people is probably the same. But their individual agendas might be very different. There needs to be underlying trust that everyone is in it for the same main goal, and they will set aside agendas."

Meera is the senior vice president of deep tech at P33 Chicago. She focuses on efforts to build the Illinois Quantum & Microelectronics Park on the Southeast Side of Chicago. Prior to P33 Chicago, Meera served as the Senior Manager, Solution Design & Program Development, at the City Tech Collaborative, and an Associate Director of Research Innovation at the University of Chicago. Her Ph.D. in chemistry is from Northwestern University.

Meera, thank you for interviewing with me. I'd like to start by learning more about your role at P33.

P33 is an economic development nonprofit. Our goal is to think about big bets that no one person or organization can do by themselves. Projects that are hard to get off the ground or are risky but present an opportunity to transform the region.

We think about how to turn our region into a top tech hub by focusing on several transformative projects. I lead our regional priorities in deep tech and science. I'm facilitating an effort to build the future of computing on the Southeast Side of Chicago, the Illinois Quantum & Microelectronics Park (IQMP). I also lead our civic user testing group, which is all our civic engagement. We believe that if you're building a big bet project, your end user will always be a resident. So, residents must have a voice.

P33 is a utility player, an intermediary. We work with industry, local government, and universities. We connect them with each other and help them speak the same language so that we can push forward.

That's exactly why I wanted to hear from you, Meera. P33's work involves many different types of organizations, and I'm sure there are many different personalities involved. I'd like to hear more about how you build trust among such a variety of players.

First, what do you do to make sure residents' voices are heard in big community projects?

There was an initiative called the City Tech Collaborative in Chicago that brought together public, private, nonprofit, and academic sectors to tackle complex city challenges. Part of that was the Civic User Testing Group, or CUT, at the City Tech Collaborative. Effectively, it was a group of about 1,600 residents at the time, across all of Chicago, who had signed up to give input on new city websites, apps, and tech. We would ask fifty or so of those residents for user testing whenever a new solution was in development. We would get them involved in the beginning, in early prototyping and later in socialization, and we paid the testers to participate.

It sounds like a model that almost any city could adopt. Thanks for sharing that!

Can you tell me more about the IQMP project?

The idea is to build a campus for quantum scale-up. Quantum has historically been a nascent-ish technology and lives in the academic world. The question is, how do we scale it up? Get industry involved? Use it as a tool to build solutions to human and business challenges?

It's a very capital-intensive field. A lot of equipment is needed. The park could provide those things and be a place where people could gather in one spot to learn and talk with each other. That's the gist. It's run by a research organization coming out of the University of Illinois, but many other groups are involved. The site is the former U.S. Steel South Works plant, and we expect our first groundbreaking before the end of 2025.

To your earlier point, how are you engaging residents in the project?

First, it's never, never soon enough to start involving people.

Second, there are community meetings that happen regularly, and a lot of folks show up.

Also, they are doing a community benefits plan. It recognizes that people living on the South Side of Chicago need jobs, and this could be a large job generator. But we also need programming to engage the next generation so that they are prepared for jobs at IQMP and related. It's a whole career pathway approach.

All along, you're trying to overcome trust issues that run deep in the community. If you're a person living on the South Side of Chicago, over the years, you have seen other people like me coming to the community and proposing projects that never happened. So, they look at me like, "Why should I believe you when those other things never worked?"

It sounds like you're coming into a community where trust has been eroded. How important is it to repair and build trust to move IQMP, or any other big initiative, forward? Scale of one to ten?

I want to say it's an eight. It's incredibly important. I struggle to give it a nine or ten because there are so many external factors. Like funding and capacity.

You know, my background is in chemistry, not economics or workforce development. I like to offer that caveat. But with that in mind, making big community projects work requires many entities coming together. The main goal among all those people is probably the same. But their individual agendas might be very different. There needs to be an underlying trust that everyone is in it for the same main goal, and they will set aside agendas.

Meera, I want to hear about your own trust-building strengths.

Authenticity and empathy are the same for me. I'm an empathetic person. I try to show up authentically and admit that I don't have all the answers. For example, I will mention that I'm not a workforce person, but I will try to do the right thing, to listen and move things forward.

It gets a little tricky when you want to hear and empathize, but you know you won't execute on everything you hear. For me, I'm honest and transparent about intentions and managing expectations.

If you're leading a community conversation and someone offers a suggestion that is impossible to do, how do you help that person feel heard without implying their idea will come to life?

I do two things. I show up authentically. My style, and this comes from me being a scientist, is to learn by asking questions. It's not because I'm being combative; it's just the way I process stuff. So, I might ask something like, "I hear you, but does that really align with what we're trying to do?"

In addition, at the top of any meeting, I state our goals so we can put ideas next to them and ask whether the ideas align with the goals.

Can you share an example of a time when this came into play?

My example relates to the National Science Foundation Regional Innovation Engines program. When it came out, everyone was excited about it. It offered a new line of funding that could add up to $160 million. Shortly after, there was the U.S. Economic Development Administration's Tech Hubs Program, which could mean up to $75 million for successful applicants. That's a lot of money, but not a whole ton when you're trying to do projects of the scale that we support.

We were in a lot of conversations where people would ask for things that we couldn't do because we just didn't have enough money, even with those big federal grants in the wings. People were disappointed, but we had to be honest. We cleared out a bunch of project ideas because, objectively, they didn't fit within the federal government's requirements.

Pointing to facts and data can help in tough conversations. It helps to put some rigor in the process, too. Like agreeing in advance on criteria for vetting ideas.

How do you maintain trust with an authority figure when you have to tell them "no"?

I might involve someone within my team who is also an authority figure so they can have a peer-to-peer conversation. Also, have an organizational structure in place so they can see that the protocol for decisions is consistent for all people, no matter their status. Finally, establish yourself as a neutral, unbiased party. Those things help.

This has been delightful, Meera! Do you have anything else to add?

I think about moments when I'm in the middle of an initiative, and people are listening to me and trusting me. I sometimes worry that I could be affected by my own biases and the information I take in. And as you go deeper into a project, you need to move things along with confidence while you continue to hear everyone. It's important to make sure you haven't surrounded yourself with others who always reinforce your point of view. To keep trust with the community, you have to zoom out and make sure you aren't missing a bunch of other perspectives, even if we aren't all in agreement.

12

BRAD LACY AND JAMIE GATES

President, CEO, and Executive Vice President, Conway Area Chamber of Commerce

Conway, Arkansas

Trust Strengths

Authenticity, Competency

"I often ask, 'Is this a problem that we can solve with money?' Sometimes a lot of money is wasted because you can't solve the problem with money alone. Trust is less expensive but more impactful."

Brad Lacy was born in Heber Springs, Arkansas, and grew up in the small Cleburne County community of Ida. A graduate of Concord High School, he moved to Conway in 1990 to attend the University of Central Arkansas. He was hired as president/CEO of the Conway Development Corporation in 2000 and added the Conway Area Chamber of Commerce to his leadership duties six years later. It marked the first time in nearly two decades that both organizations would be led by the same individual.

Brad's greatest professional achievements are his team, their work, and their two-time National Chamber of the Year awards. In 2012, Governor Mike Beebe appointed Brad to a seven-year term on the University of Central Arkansas Board of Trustees, marking a full-circle moment for the first-generation college graduate.

With his great love of toads, wampus cats, and purple bears, Brad is often mistaken for a Conway native. When not promoting his adopted hometown, he enjoys traveling and living life with his friends and family.

Jamie Gates is an economic developer and nonprofit executive based in Conway, Arkansas, currently serving as the executive vice president for the Conway Area Chamber of Commerce and the Conway Development Corporation. With over twenty-five years of experience, he has successfully landed billion-dollar projects, from paper mills to hyperscale data centers, worked with multiple Fortune 100 companies, and led efforts to finance and build hundreds of millions of dollars' worth of job-creating infrastructure. Jamie holds a degree in finance from the University of Central Arkansas and is a Certified Chamber Executive.

Brad and Jamie, thanks for agreeing to this twofer interview. I have seen both of you in action and believe you are a dynamic duo of trust-building. Conway is as much fun as it is future-focused.

My experiences in Conway were part of the inspiration for this book. I think you all are an example of how to not only build trust but also strengthen it year after year. Kudos to you and your team!

BRAD: Thank you for telling us that. That's very encouraging in the line of work we do. We spend a lot of time building relationships, so it's just nice to hear that someone notices that paying off.

I want to dig into specific things that y'all do to grow those relationships and camaraderie. But first, I want to hear your thoughts on this topic overall. On a scale of one to ten, how important is trust in Conway's success as a community?

BRAD: Yes, it's a ten. Not just for Conway but for everyone. They just need to stick with it for the long haul.

JAMIE: It took forty months for us to secure one of our recent projects. That requires trust from our board members, investors, and others in the community. They trust us to know we're doing the right thing and that these things don't happen overnight.

Have you ever had a project that required you to quickly build trust?

JAMIE: It helps when personalities line up. Recently, a company was looking at Conway as a possible new location. The decision maker came in and wanted to move fast. We didn't have an NDA in place. The question was, can we dispense with legal formalities? If we can't, then you're not people I can trust. An NDA won't fix that. That was one of our best professional experiences.

BRAD: One of the things we always try to do is establish that trust by talking about our experience. Not in a bragging way, but more like, we're professionals and have experience with projects like yours, big public companies, build-to-suit leasebacks, whatever else. It helps establish trust because this isn't our first rodeo.

I've heard from several people that trust is nothing without strategy. How do you feel about that?

JAMIE: That hits me in the wrong way. What good is a strategy without trust? When we get the right five people on a team who all trust each other, we can make it up along the way. Strategies are nice, but it's hard to predict the future. You've got to be nimble, which means you have to set egos aside, too.

I often ask, "Is this a problem that we can solve with money?" Sometimes, a lot of money is wasted because you can't solve the problem with money alone. Trust is less expensive but more impactful.

You're getting into it, but can we talk about your trust-building strengths? I shared a list of eight Trust Strengths to consider.

JAMIE: I think we're authentic. Sometimes, someone can be so professional that it comes off as being disingenuous. People might think, *You don't act like this at home or when I'm not around. What else can I not trust you over?*

BRAD: Our revenue model makes us different because we don't accept any public money. We hustle because we don't get a big check from local governments. Is hustle a strength?

Good suggestion. Maybe hustle should be a Trust Builder strength!

BRAD: We ask for our budget one dollar at a time from all our private investors. We start at zero and ask for that again every year. We better have something to prove the value of their investment. That's part of the relationship-building process. We're touching base with these folks regularly and reminding them of what we're doing with the money they are investing.

It's unusual to find an economic development initiative that's completely privately funded. Does that make you more agile?

JAMIE: Yes and yes. We say that taking public money makes you soft. It helps us relate to businesses better.

Can you share some tips on building trust with other local leaders?

JAMIE: This is going to feel self-evident, but one way to build trust is to be honest, and being honest is different from not lying. Being honest means, "Here's the data. This is how we stack up for good and bad." Economic developers and chambers that just sell and promote just the good things aren't being entirely honest. It erodes trust when you don't use data and when you don't share the flaws along with the strengths. Like, on a community tour, I'll show our best neighborhoods and our worst ones.

BRAD: I agree. Sometimes, people get upset that we're not always 100 percent positive, but we love this place as much as they do. We're bought in and love it enough to be honest about the things we need to change. Instead of crying, hiding, and being mad at each other, let's lock arms and figure out how to solve problems.

Yes, I've worked with places that have gained a lot by showing their flaws alongside their strengths. No place is perfect.

BRAD: Also, Amy, you mentioned that you've never seen trust-building line-itemed in an economic development budget. But we do. For example, we spend money getting our leaders in front of our delegation in DC every year. Those trips also help people get to know each other and dream. Trust is a byproduct of their time together.

Another thing that we do well is building social fabric.

Tell me more about ways to build social fabric. I like that term.

BRAD: We create purposeful opportunities for people to come together and experience the same thing at the same time. It's like our Toad Suck Daze event—crazy name, I know. But it creates a shared experience for our community that becomes part of our story.

I have to mention that I saw someone wearing a Toad Suck Daze polo shirt in a hotel lobby while I was traveling abroad. I immediately knew where he was from.

A Conway ambassador! Our Christmas tree lighting has the same effect. It's like a Hallmark movie with 3,000 attendees. It doesn't matter if you're Republican, Democrat, gay, straight, Black, white, rich, poor… everyone can participate.

You know, some people in our profession just want to do deals. That's an important part of this job. But building a community physically and socially is the most important part of what we do because that allows us to do the deals.

You're talking about a culture of self-reliance. Can you point to a person or project that has sparked that culture?

JAMIE: The origin of the chamber was in 1891, when Captain W.W. Martin wanted the town to expand economically. His idea was to go after higher ed. He established the chamber to raise money to get the first college. They were successful. And then they got the second one. And then the third. That approach continued early on with getting sewer infrastructure in 1911, broadband in 1996, and so on.

I've met some great storytellers in Conway, including you two. How does that play out today with social media and all the noise?

JAMIE: Local daily newspapers were especially big in cities our size, but some have gone down to just a few times a week or morphed into the larger metro's news. Still, you need to tell your own story and be proactive. When a local newspaper only publishes a few times a week, you start to lose civic literacy. People don't read about the planning commission, but they might hear about it secondhand. Or, we might have an exciting announcement on a Tuesday, but the newspaper prints the story on Saturday. I think it's exciting, but by the time it's in print, there is nothing but crickets.

BRAD: Yes. It means that we tell the story ourselves, and we don't depend on the media. The best way is the harder way. If you're talking about trust, it takes time. I mean, we have a large social media following, but it took years to build that. Years of useful content.

Before we go, is there anything else you'd like to share?

JAMIE: People in Conway believe that anything is possible, and that is part of our secret sauce. We've defied odds for more than a hundred years. There's a self-reliance that doesn't depend on other people to do things. We problem-solve for ourselves. It's part of the DNA here.

I've had the opportunity to experience Conway's spirit of positivity firsthand. Please keep it going for the next 100 years.

13
ROSE FAGLER

Economic Development Manager, Weyerhaeuser

Fernandina Beach, Florida

Trust Strengths

Authenticity, Active listening

"Some of the projects we're involved with might take thirty years to complete. We're working on such a large scale that we need to take it one small bite at a time. If you deliver on your promise and make sure the work doesn't collapse local capacity, even if it's a small step in a grand plan, it builds trust."

Rose Fagler takes on big, hairy, audacious projects, building departments and high-performing teams, and getting everyone across the finish line successfully. She is responsible for economic development for Weyerhaeuser's real estate developments, providing vision and market strategy and shaping the success of development sites.

Prior to Weyerhaeuser, Rose served on the Progress Energy Florida team, siting a new nuclear energy complex with two hundred miles of baseload transmission. She also established a full-service marketing and communications department for Gainesville Regional Utilities and ran the national employee sales incentives departments for the Lane Bryant and Structure brand divisions of The Limited, Inc.

Rose has served on the foundation boards of the Cade Museum of Creativity & Invention, the Frostburg State University Foundation, the University of West Florida Haas Center, the Florida Economic Development Council, and the University of Florida Institute of Food and Agricultural Sciences Public Issues Education Center.

In 2020, Rose launched the Strong Women Network, providing peer-to-peer mentoring for women in business leadership roles. Rose is a graduate of Frostburg State University and was named one of the university's Distinguished Alumni in 2020–2021.

Rose, trust among local leaders is a topic that has been on my mind since we worked together fifteen or so years ago. I feel fortunate to have seen your trust-building work in person. You are gifted in forging community trust across lines. People can learn a lot from you.

You know, reviewing your questions for this interview made me sit down and reflect. I realized that sometimes things that seem intuitive to me are what's needed to build a community.

Trust plays a huge role. You're not getting anywhere without it.

After five years, the project that we worked on together did not come to fruition, even though some of the best minds in the country were on the team. I don't want to call it out, but let's just say the project would have resulted in one of the largest R&D-centered, live-work-play developments in the country.

It came down to local politics. In this interview, I would like to explore those specific lessons as well as hear your overall thoughts on the topic of trust building.

Let's start with a softball question. On a scale of one to ten, please rate the importance of trust among local community leaders in economic development.

It's a ten-plus. Really, there is no real scale. You've got to build trust. And it takes a long time.

In the project we worked on together, Amy, it took three and a half years to form that foundation of trust, and we did so very intentionally and transparently. From the beginning of our work there, we committed to respecting local residents, always doing the right thing, and being hyper-inclusive.

Rose, I've done this work for three decades, and I can't recall another process that was as patient and thoughtful as the one you all led.

I'm jumping right into this. Do you remember a turning point in the project where progress started stalling and the dialogue turned negative?

Yes, it was around the time when boomers were getting on social media. I remember the exact month and year. Before that moment, the project would have been approved. Then a couple of things started happening. There was a social media group that took us by surprise.

At first, older generations were joining social media to stay in touch with their kids and friends. We were all reconnecting, and it was glorious. Then, right about the time our project was moving ahead, folks realized that they could use the social media façade and say whatever they wanted. The trolls were getting likes.

They started feeling empowered, emboldened to come out from behind Facebook and stand behind the microphone at local council meetings. Sometimes, they said the most outlandish and racist things. They believed they were doing good for the community, and that justified the horrible things they were communicating.

One of the local officials was a board member of a chapter of a large environmental group. The organizers began to bus in people from outside the area who weren't familiar with the community but who answered an email or social media post. They would show up at council meetings and pressure the swing vote against our project. They started getting abusive and threatening.

And I was one of their targets.

Why you, Rose, when there were so many other people involved in the project?

They saw me as the linchpin in building trust. They saw that if they could take out one Trust Builder, then everything else would go down.

Things got so targeted and risky for me that I had to change churches, salons, dentists, you name it. My family and I eventually moved.

Is there a risk in being a Trust Builder?

I'd rather lead from behind. If there's a void in leadership, I'll fill in. But I prefer to be behind the scenes, surrounded by people full of wisdom and experience.

It can be easier for a Trust Builder if the people around them step out in front of the community when push comes to shove, if they back you up.

When you have real folks who want to do what's right and are thinking for future generations, that builds trust. Leaders who work at that level are going to risk having something blow back on them because some people are afraid of change.

Rose, I'd like to shift gears and talk about your own approach to being a Trust Builder. I shared eight Trust Strengths for you to consider.

First, being authentic. If you meet me at work or in the grocery store or at church, you'll get who I am. There's just not enough time in the day to be five different people. If someone asks me a question, I will answer them directly, even if they may not like the answer.

And that requires you to actively listen to people. Observe them so you really hear what they say. When I understand people, I want to do the right thing.

We engaged a facilitator once who came to our public meetings and captured comments on paper. He would sometimes draw pictures and hold eight Sharpies in his hands as he worked.

I remember him. We called him "Edward Marker Hands" because he was so super-skilled.

Haha! His work showed people that they were heard. He captured their thoughts visually. Then, the next time we met, we would play back what he captured so that, again, people could know that we listened.

There's another trust trait that's not on your list, and that's never over-promising.

Don't overpromise. That's a good tip, for sure!

Some of the projects we're involved in might take thirty years to complete. We're working on such a large scale that we need to take it one small bite at a time. As soon as you show them the long-term vision, it can be overwhelming. That's a greater leap for them to make from the trust perspective.

If you deliver on your promise and make sure the work doesn't collapse local capacity, even if it's a small step in a grand plan, it builds trust. Then rinse and repeat.

You're touching on another question. What advice would you share with someone who wants to improve their ability to build trust with other local leaders?

Invite people in. And feed them.

When we did community engagement for one of our big projects, we involved a great caterer. In every meeting, people would arrive to a spread of delicious food. Some of them who opposed the project would arrive with arms crossed and say, "I refuse to eat your food."

So, I would say, "That's fine. I hope you don't mind if we eat. It is lunchtime." We would start eating and talking, and the next thing you knew, they would try a cookie. And then the chicken salad or whatever. You could see the barriers coming down as people shared a meal. And while we ate, we would answer their questions without dancing around topics.

I think the best thing to do is meet people right where they are. You have to go out and meet the people who are either going to benefit from or be negatively impacted by a project. You need to hear their concerns and desires, then shape the outcome so they can see themselves in the work.

14

RANDY THELEN

President and CEO, **The Right Place, Inc.**

Grand Rapids, Michigan

Trust Strengths

Authenticity, Empathy, Transparency

"If you want a high-performing, high-quality region, you've got to find a way to stretch out. Trust allows you to do that."

As president and CEO of The Right Place, Randy Thelen leads the economic development strategy for the Greater Grand Rapids Region. Since taking the helm in 2021, the organization has supported the creation and retention of 4,000+ jobs and $1billion+ in new capital investment for the region. Randy has expanded the organization's initiatives to include community development, placemaking, and talent. He championed the launch of a ten-year regional tech strategy that positions the region as one of the leading tech hubs in the Midwest.

Randy joined The Right Place team in 2021 after serving as senior vice president of economic development at the Downtown Denver

Partnership. There, he supported downtown projects totaling more than $1 billion in investments. Prior to that, Randy led the Greater Omaha Economic Development Partnership, a two-state, eight-county regional economic development effort. His career began in Evart and Monroe, Michigan, before he moved to the Michigan Economic Development Corporation (MEDC). His Master of Arts in Applied Economics is from Binghamton University, and his Bachelor of Arts in Economics is from Alma College.

Randy, I'm leading these Trust Builder interviews with leaders I admire in the field, so of course, I thought of you. How important is trust among local leaders in economic development? Scale of one to ten?

On a scale of one to ten, it's very high. A nine or ten. We work on projects that might not otherwise get done. We're trying to make things happen that go above and beyond the basic efforts that happen routinely in communities.

That means the community has to stretch out. If there's not a high degree of trust among local leaders, it will be much more difficult. The community will just settle for the normal. If you want a high-performing, high-quality region, you've got to find a way to stretch higher. Trust allows you to do that.

It's literally like a trust fall. At the start of a big community project, economic developers are often the first involved. We need to feel confident that if we pursue it and fall backwards, the community will be there to catch us.

As you're talking, I'm thinking about the speed of projects. Some of what you do is long-range and visionary. But other opportunities come up that might only have a three- or four-month window.

When you think about companies today that are looking for a location for their next expansion, they are waiting longer to make decisions, but they aren't changing their opening dates. It's compressing timelines for local leaders, which means there needs to be some existing level of trust.

I've been exploring trust among community leaders, but do you think local trust plays a role in a company's mind when choosing its next location?

Yes, 100 percent. They are looking at all the local leaders. They're trying to grow their business to the next level, and they're looking for a community that they can trust will help them get there.

What are some ways that leaders in Grand Rapids foster trust with each other? What would someone from the outside observe about the interaction of leaders around the region?

For one, rarely do we sign a nondisclosure agreement. We expect the companies to trust us with their information, and it doesn't require a legal document to do so. So, that's a signal that we value trust.

We typically have dozens of local leaders actively engaged in courting a company to locate here. That itself can show that we are a trusting community. And we are a team of people who will work together.

We look for the same in the company, considering Grand Rapids. Our expectation is if someone will expand their business here, we don't want them to just come in and take. We want them to be part of the community, to bring something that makes us better. Trust is two-way.

I'd like to learn more about you. I shared eight different Trust Strengths. Which ones seem most like Randy?

I can see myself in all of them, but I thought authenticity and being transparent, with empathy, resonated with me.

You've been with The Right Place for more than four years now. When you joined, how did you build trust with other local leaders?

Being myself from the beginning. The staff, the business community, and civic leadership all need to know who you are as a person. I try to build authentic relationships. It wasn't easy starting the CEO role in the middle of COVID. But in a weird way, the social distancing and online meetings let me meet more people quickly. In my first hundred days, I was able to meet with five times the number of people I would have otherwise.

To break down barriers, my wife and I started inviting people into our home. If we're planning a dinner with leaders around town or staff, we bring them to our house for a picnic. It helps everyone let their guard down. They can see how I live and my teenagers in their full glory.

That's special, Randy. I'm sure it deepens relationships. Are there other specific things you do to build trust with other local leaders?

It's not necessarily specific, but it's a mindset. I lead with trust. When I meet someone, I instantly trust that they are a good person, do their best, and make good decisions. I never start off thinking someone has bad intentions.

It goes back to my study of economics. It's the assumption that people act in their own self-interest. And if you think in those terms, then they are doing what's good for them, not trying to harm you.

Through that viewpoint, there comes understanding and empathy. And 99.9 percent of the time, people reciprocate.

When you talk about self-interest, people might jump to personal agendas and think that's a deterrent to trust.

Everyone has agendas, right? Think about elected officials. They ran for a particular reason. I want to know their motivation. People think that they are running for elected office for an ego trip, but nine times out of ten, it's some passion project that they couldn't move through normal channels. Like connecting trails or repairing roads. They're trying to fix it from the inside.

Can we think about times before and after social media and how that has changed things? Does it impact the baseline of trust?

Today, trust has to be extended further and further into the community, and that's being tested. Say a new company comes to town, and they bring new jobs, tax investment, and all the multiplier effects. If you're in a leadership role, you can see those benefits. But if you're

John Q. Public, living three blocks away from the new company and not going to get a job there or benefit, you might only see the negative externalities. Maybe it's a fear of increased traffic or losing co-workers who go to work there.

I mentioned social media, but that bleeds into the subject of public hearings at local government, like city council meetings.

Yes. Those public hearing processes are designed so that government officials can hear from the public. But they don't. They hear from the most vocal people.

I think we need to do a better job of building trust across the broader community and responding to the public. Elected officials listen at those meetings, but they don't provide answers or express their opinions in those settings. It's the format of the meetings. Nobody gets a quick answer on the spot, so frustration builds. And then the next person gets more agitated. It snowballs.

That's an issue in many communities. What can be done about it?

We're trying to get ahead of it here. Prior to a public meeting, we're hosting town hall meetings. We put four or five stations in a big room. We have a person at each station who has some expertise on the topics and can answer questions on infrastructure, traffic, employment, environment, and whatever other topics might pop up. People attending those can have their questions answered. Then, at the public meeting, they can express their concerns or why they are excited, but they don't need to ask more questions.

Who organizes those meetings?

The Right Place and the local jurisdiction. It's a posted meeting.

I applaud you. It takes courage to open up the process like that.

If I put on my empathetic hat, it can be a healthy reminder that not everyone likes change. As a professional, I know that growth is a positive force, and decline is a brutal situation for any community. Growth can create challenges, but those are 1000 percent better than the challenges that are facing communities that are in decline.

I think that's the next thing for our profession. The days of rapid announcements followed by the high school marching band celebrating these projects are in a moment of pause. We've got to find a way to do it in a different way, which means more public engagement and transparent communication.

Community leaders seem to be in a new realm of being more visible than ever while having to expand their reach to the bigger community, including people who don't understand how the dots connect.

It comes back to our kids and grandkids. Do we want them to be able to live near us and find good opportunities? A healthy, thriving community? Yes, of course we do.

Before we end, Randy, what advice do you give your team on trust building?

I try to model it. I'm a transparent leader, so we're an open book on finances and personnel management. I also try to be myself and encourage them to be their authentic selves. There are leaders at every level of an organization, not just by title. We have a great culture here, but I'm not always around. For culture to thrive, everyone has to have ownership in it.

15

JOHN HULL

Executive Director, Roanoke Regional Partnership

Roanoke, Virginia

Trust Strengths

Competency, Authenticity, Transparency

"Speed can make or break. And mistrust is the detriment of speed. Fear stymies any ability to get creative. Sometimes, you have to do the bold thing even if there are risks. That's much easier if you live in a high-trust community."

As executive director at Roanoke Regional Partnership and Western Virginia Regional Industrial Facility Authority, John has over twenty years of experience in economic development, with a focus on regional projects involving multiple governments and stakeholders. He is a Certified Economic Research Professional (CERP) and a recognized leader in the field of economic development, having received awards such as North America's Top 50 Economic Developers and 40 Under 40.

John specializes in organizational leadership, real estate development, and project management, with skills in fundraising, strategic planning, public relations, site development, demographic data and research, economic development marketing, deal structuring, applied economic research, economic impact analysis, program development, grant writing, and communication. His mission is to foster economic growth and innovation in the Roanoke region by leveraging its assets and opportunities and creating a vibrant, prosperous community for all.

Thank you so much for interviewing with me! We've worked together on two strategies and other projects for the Roanoke area. I appreciate the way you bring people together there, so I'm looking forward to your thoughts on this topic.

I've noticed that communities with high degrees of trust among local leaders are the ones that outperform others. It might sound like a no-brainer, but I need to truth-test this, John. Am I off my rocker?

No. It's really interesting. Because, as you said, you kind of take it for granted. But I think that's also how communities fall into the trap. Of course, trust is important, but a lot of folks don't evaluate where they are on this or understand what it means.

Trust is a ten out of ten in terms of importance to economic development. It's just absolutely crucial. It's a team sport. Having successful community projects requires working in collaboration with a cast of hundreds. It involves public and private sectors, utilities, economic developers, educators, et cetera. Everyone has a role. They need to stay in their lane and do their role while trusting others to do their job.

Community leaders need to work at the pace of business. If different parts of the community aren't talking or collaborating, you're going to fail based on speed alone.

A cast of hundreds. That's a lot of trust to foster.

Yes. I think of Google's recent decision to invest here. We had a lot of socialization to do around that project. Companies like that can experience pushback. NIMBY-ism. And we had to involve a large cast of local leaders. That created a huge disclosure risk, and we trusted everyone to keep details confidential. Ultimately, we had zero leakage.

That's a powerful indicator of trust, John. Wow. Do you think trust increases flexibility and speed?

Speed can make or break an opportunity. And mistrust is a detriment to speed. Say someone needs to socialize something now, but they're afraid that they will get fired. Fear stymies any ability to get creative because they're constantly having to comply with stuff.

Sometimes, you have to do the bold thing even if there are risks. That's much easier if you live in a high-trust community.

I'm exploring the strengths of Trust Builders like you. Of the list of eight Trust Strengths that I sent you, which ones are unique to John?

I think competency is big for me. And authenticity. Certainly, they're not the only ones. You know, a meaningful connection is huge, so you need to communicate often and regularly.

I wonder if enthusiasm should be one as well. Enthusiasm for the mission and a sincere belief that the region can do this. It's critical to building support. Maybe that's a dimension of authenticity?

Totally agree, John. So many times, you need someone in the room to be completely enthusiastic about a project to get other people to follow along.

Yes. Recently, we had a big project opportunity. It was bigger than we ever contemplated, and we were very enthusiastic about it. We only had a week to come up with a proposal that involved a multi-jurisdictional site, incentives, and new infrastructure with multiple providers. Without trust and positivity, fundamentally, there was no way that we could get people together and deliver an innovative proposal in that timeframe.

We didn't win that project, but it formed roots that helped us with several other major successes. Sometimes, losses are the foundation for future wins.

Another interviewee said that her trust-building skills have evolved over time. How about you?

Showing up consistently is key at all stages of your career. If you aren't present, you're not thought of. Raise your hand so that people know you're out there.

Same with following through and executing. That means keeping people updated. We do a lot of texting, conference calls, and face-to-face meetings. Our private funders and government folks get together quarterly. In those meetings, I provide them with thoughtful content and an opportunity to react and share their opinions.

I'm curious. You came from a research background. Do you think that helped in your position as a trusted leader in the region?

As the partnership's research director before I stepped into my current role, I had a long runway to exhibit and display technical ability. A lot of other local leaders already had experience working with me. Trust is something you build over time. Being an objective voice, providing truth, by way of data, is incredibly helpful. Sometimes, the news isn't good, but folks know that you'll deliver the truth, and that builds trust.

So many community meetings are one-directional. Careful work goes into what's presented, but it's a presentation, not a dialogue. As an observer, I want to say, "You have fifty of your greatest local leaders in one room. Why aren't you asking them for their ideas?"

Yes, a missed opportunity. Sometimes, people are afraid of the answers. That's a trust issue, too. They aren't comfortable with the uncertainty of what might come up.

I think you must be open. I have found it only to be productive. I have never regretted opening it up for input.

I know your region has seen a lot of change in leadership lately. Building trust with new leaders is a topic that's been on my mind. How do you maintain a consistent commitment to community development even through those changes?

Yes, the private sector is stable in terms of leadership, but public sector leadership continues to change. It means you put more effort into elected officials and government administrators. It makes the job a little harder, but it's critical. This is a team sport.

What percentage of your time today is spent meeting with your local leaders? How much is spent internally versus out in the market?

I'd say it's 5 to 10 percent. It just needs to be more intentional in terms of getting together.

You have a great team and a lot of ground to cover. What advice do you offer your team members on building trust?

I tell folks to listen and remember that it's usually better if the idea doesn't come from you all the time. You need to plant the seed. It's a lot more powerful if you have champions who will own your idea and advance it. It's not about my team personally getting credit; it's about making a difference in the community.

Letting others get the spotlight when there is a community win is a theme of my interviews.

It's tricky, right? Because the announcement of a win is what enables you to do the work. It fuels resources and political buy-in. People need to know you're working. When we're making an announcement, I like to say, "This is a result of our partners and their investment. It is a result of a cast of hundreds who pulled this together. It is not about a single guy or gal. Literally, the whole community did this."

Beyond you and the team, how do other leaders in the region build trust with each other?

By being present. Showing up: lunches, coffees, things like that. Handshakes. Those little actions are most important.

John, any parting words of wisdom?

Everyone in our field should be reading this book, Amy. I hope so. How powerful could this be, communicating this concept? I've been thinking about the role of trust in our work for a long time, so I really appreciate you doing this. I think it's critical.

I hope so! Thank you for the encouragement!

16

TIM GIULIANI

President and CEO, Orlando Regional Partnership

Orlando, Florida

Trust Strengths

Competency, Empathy

"Trust is certainly a critical ingredient, but there are others, too. Even if there is trust, if there isn't alignment of goals, you could run into trouble. Alignment is important."

Tim Giuliani is a national leader in growing cities that deliver economic growth. His approach is centered on the powerful idea that by investing in creating places people want to live in and visit, communities will attract companies where people want to work and thrive.

As president and CEO of the Orlando Economic Partnership, he has led efforts that have helped attract over 30,000 new jobs, $3.6 billion in capital investment, and $3.3 billion in annual payroll. Tim's collaborative work with elected, higher education, and private sector leaders led to the investment of $500 million in the Florida semiconductor cluster.

Giuliani's work to position Orlando as a global, creative capital is focused on cultivating civic leadership and bringing those leaders together to align around the long-term opportunities and challenges that face the region.

We've chatted about this book and my premise that trust among leaders directly impacts economic development. How does that resonate with you?

Trust is certainly a critical ingredient, but there are others, too. Even if there is trust, if there isn't alignment of goals, you could run into trouble. Alignment is important.

And so is whether people are concerned about who gets credit. If a local leader wants all the credit, it can kill progress. I've seen situations where an elected official didn't involve the business community in a major referendum because he thought it would take credit away from him, and the referendum didn't pass.

When that's the case, with something so hotly political, how can an economic development organization or chamber play a role without taking sides?

Point to the facts. From a trust standpoint, put the facts out there and allow some of the opinions to go away.

You're in a fast-growing region in a state where politics sometimes make the headlines. What are a few of your personal trust-building strengths of the eight that I shared with you?

I keep going back to StrengthsFinder, which isn't exactly what you have here.

That's okay. Tell me about those.

Strategic and visionary. I can see the big picture and anticipate where things are going. I'm surrounded by good people who are great at execution, well-connected, and empathetic. We all serve important roles. It's a well-rounded team.

Tim, you've mentioned that structures themselves can either support trust or lead to distrust. Can you elaborate? Are you talking politics?

Obviously, different national and state administrations can either support or become major detriments to economic development. Even at the local level, you can get people on the county commission or a city council who are anti-growth. And those people might not trust each other, or their staff members might not like each other. Things can get paralyzed. That might be your next book, Amy.

I'm always open to ideas. Personalities aside, are there policies or structures baked into local systems that exacerbate trust challenges?

In Florida, we have sunshine laws that require meetings, records, correspondence, and other actions to be open to the public. It can be challenging, especially in economic development when companies need some level of confidentiality when they are making site decisions.

Also, we're one of three counties in Florida with a mayor at the county level who is elected at large. Everyone else is elected by district. That means that the mayor is a powerful position. Their staff members are, then, also powerful, impacting trust by either being open and consistent or lacking the willingness to collaborate. So much depends on the individual personalities.

I could imagine that the wrong person could make it a bit of a sh*t show, to use a technical term.

Right!

I'd like to learn about the culture of trust in the Orlando region. I led a strategy there in the late 1990s and remember there being a ton of energy and optimism.

This region is different from other places. You don't have to grow up in Orlando or be a part of a certain company or wear a suit and tie. There's such a welcoming culture here. If you're interested, sign up, and we'll take you.

We have a lot of people working together. All the big projects that have happened here have been regional or multi-government. Like SunRail, for example, and we're working on expanding it. The project development study is funded by Universal, the Florida Department of Transportation, the City of Orlando, Orange County, Seminole County, Osceola County... you get the picture. They all contributed to the study, and then we all went to DC together to advocate for the investment.

It's interesting to hear that all three counties participated, since the SunRail tracks weren't physically going through Osceola County. What motivated them to join the other regional partners?

We pulled together data about people who live in Osceola County and who work in Orange County and took that information to their county commissioner. Our research showed that 20 percent of their residents have jobs in Orange County. It comes down to that: have good information, and the right decision can be made.

Overall, we just think and act regionally. Another example is our Major League Soccer team. They are in the city of Orlando, but the men's training facility is in Osceola County to the south, and the women's training facility is to the north in Seminole. Like the partnership, our sports commission works regionally.

Tim, you've had the opportunity to lead chambers in several states. Can you tell me about someone you've met along the way who was a true Trust Builder and what lessons they taught you?

I think of Harvey Schmidt, whom I followed at the Raleigh Chamber. He is retired now, but I recommend you interview him. Harvey is hands down the best I've ever seen at this job. He's number one.

I will interview him. Thanks for the recommendation. What exactly does he do to make him the best?

Practically everything. For example, he held a monthly breakfast with the county manager, city manager, and superintendent. I continued the tradition and added the mayor, head of the community college, and someone from NC State. We would meet at the chamber office and go around the table, saying what we're each working on and what help we needed.

We repeated that approach with several other groups, like a monthly luncheon with the chamber president, tourism president, and downtown alliance president. Even when things got dicey between two of the partners at the table, they had time in those meetings to go back and forth with each other in a constructive way, with the rest of us there in support. That was critical to knowing each other and trusting each other.

Harvey also led an annual leadership mission to another city every single year, and it paid off. Like when we sat down for our first finance committee meeting to discuss funding the transportation ballot referendum. The entire table had ridden bus rapid transit in, like, five other cities already. When we started raising money for the campaign, we were starting from third base. Everyone knew each other. Everyone traveled with each other and knew exactly what we were talking about. They were well-informed.

We met for eighteen months every Friday at three o'clock in our conference room to work on the campaign. We opened the tent to include the unions, the Black churches, the Sierra Club, AARP, bicycle advocates, and others… you get the point. The referendum passed because all those diverse leaders were calling on their own constituents.

We instituted leadership missions in Orlando, too. We've gone to Pittsburgh, Minneapolis, Denver, Nashville, and Charlotte this year. While we are there to learn, if nothing else, we get three days with many of the top leaders to get to know each other. We don't over-schedule to give people downtime together. It's not a boondoggle; we do have goals around giving people time to connect versus hearing from one speaker after another.

17
CHRIS PUMPHREY

President, Elevate Douglas Economic Partnership

Douglasville, Georgia

Trust Strengths

Competency, Reliability, Active listening

"You start by understanding what people believe and why. What's undergirding their belief? For most people, their vision isn't unattainable. It just might be how it's presented. Once you understand what's driving their position, you can match those interests to your own vision."

At the time of our interview, Chris was leading the charge at the Elevate Douglas Economic Partnership, drawing on over fourteen years of experience in economic and community development. His mission at Elevate was to foster a sustainable economy, an endeavor that balanced community interests with strategic real estate development. The heart of his work lies in cultivating relationships and pioneering policies that nurture economic growth.

Chris's tenure has been marked by a strong commitment to public service and strategic planning, leveraging skills in real estate and community leadership to drive change. In collaboration with local government and businesses, Chris and the Elevate team constructed a cohesive vision for progress. The culmination of these efforts is not only a reflection of his dedication but also the collective drive of the community towards continuous development and prosperity.

Chris, thank you for agreeing to an interview. What do you think about this topic of trust among local leaders and economic development? On a scale of one to ten, how important is it?

I went through your questions, and this was one I struggled with the most. I started thinking about how you define success. I'm ultimately coming to ten out of ten. But in some cases, you need success to build trust. Then, as it builds, you're able to do more.

Some people might believe that if they have a win or two, then they're successful. In that case, trust is a five or six on the scale. For others who are trying to transform a community, then it's a ten.

I can see that. It depends on the person's goals. How do you build more trust if someone doesn't prioritize economic development?

That could burn out some economic developers. Some communities just need someone to go out and recruit more businesses. Others need someone who is willing to ride through that and focus on more holistic community development. It's really important that the person believes in the community's potential to build trust over time.

You're a transformation-focused leader, Chris. I've seen you in action when we led the first Elevate strategy and supported you with updates.

I started working here fifteen years ago.

Sometimes, change might not happen at the pace that others want, but I remind them that our community is two hundred years old. It's going to be here beyond us. We're here for a moment in time, and we have an opportunity to make a positive impact.

You sent another question about a time when trust played a significant role in a win, but I don't want to jump ahead of your questions.

Yes, let's jump around the questions! I would love to hear your example.

When I started at the Development Authority of Douglas County (DADC), we had two different development authorities: ours and the other one at the City of Douglasville. I had the trust of the assistant city manager, and she saw that I was listening and wanted to do good for the community without selfish interests. She trusted me and the team. That trust opened the door for the city and county to consolidate economic development efforts into one organization.

That led to us hiring your firm, Avalanche, to do our first-ever strategic plan and then to create our current private partnership, Elevate Douglas.

Over the next ten years, Douglas County outpaced the Atlanta region and the state in wage growth. It started with that trusting relationship.

That is music to my ears! And back to the assistant city manager (who is now the current city manager), how specifically did you establish that relationship with her and others?

One of the reasons my board hired me was because they wanted me to improve relationships between the county and city. So, I knew it was my objective. I had been working at the state level and seen how different communities across Georgia did economic and community development. I knew where it really worked and who was struggling.

I started by meeting with people and hearing their concerns. And I reiterated that it wasn't in our best interest to be divided as a community. I listened to what they wanted the community to be, and I presented ideas on how we could get there. I looked for things that we could do together. The city manager saw it very clearly and isn't partisan in how she does things. We think alike and have a shared background in community development. It's still a great collaboration.

Taking a step back, you said that the first thing that you did was listen to people. That's a strength. What are a few of your other strengths as a Trust Builder?

I'm a consensus builder. It's a strength and a little bit of a weakness at times. I'm also a visionary. That's what drew me to Douglas County in the first place. I saw a community that had the natural makeup to be successful.

It's the combination of those two things that has carried us through. It wasn't just listening and collecting notes, but it was also casting a vision of where we could be.

Was it difficult to convince people of that vision when you were so new to town?

You don't do that right off the bat. But I had legitimacy coming in with a statewide perspective. I knew how state leaders viewed the county.

Chris, what advice would you give to a team member or young professional who wants to be a better Trust Builder?

There's a lot of self-awareness. You need to know your core beliefs and your negotiables and non-negotiables. It's not just listening to hear what others say and being a yes man. It's figuring out how you, as an individual, can best contribute to that other person or organization. How can I bring value versus gain from them?

Self-awareness is also knowing that you don't have all the answers. I have been told that I do a great job of making a point without over-stating it to the level where the other person feels attacked.

You have a gift for allowing quietness in the conversation. I admire that about you. But what if you really need to make a point that's contradictory to another local leader's view?

You start by understanding what they believe and why. What's under-girding their belief? For most people, their vision isn't far off or unat-tainable. It just might be how it's presented. Once you understand what's driving their position, you can match those interests to your own vision. If there's complete misalignment, then we might need to pivot and go someplace else.

Chris, what do other local leaders do to build trust with each other? Your examples can be very granular. In fact, those are helpful.

Our chamber president and I started meeting regularly with our mayor and chairperson. We talk through anything and everything. I give them an update on our strategic priorities so that they're informed and comfortable speaking about things when they are out in public.

Also, I have a graphic that shows a wheel of economic sustainability. How it works and all the different ingredients at play. We're a cog in the wheel but not the whole wheel. There are other factors, like quality amenities, housing, talent, retail, etc. It's all connected, and every element is important. I use that graphic as a basis for many of our talks.

Maybe trust can wrap around the graphic?

You can't have the wheel without trust.

18
BRANDON DENNISON

Co-Founder and Executive President, Coalfield Development Corporation

Marshall, West Virginia

Trust Strengths

Empathy, Consistency

"I was raised in a family of good storytellers and conversationalists. I feel like I can foster relationships through storytelling. I have genuine empathy, even with people with different belief systems from my own, by showing up reliably. Here, we've had the rug pulled out from underneath folks for a long time, and it can be hard to break through those promises being broken. So, you have to consistently show up and keep showing up."

Brandon is Ashley Dennison's husband and the father of their boys, Owen and Will. A lifelong West Virginian, he is the founder and CEO of Coalfield Development, which works to rebuild the Appalachian economy from the ground up. Coalfield has invested in more than 92 new social enterprises and trained more than four thousand unemployed or underemployed workers.

Believing in the power of collective impact, Brandon co-founded the Appalachian Community Transformation Now Coalition (ACT Now) along with dozens of other businesses and organizations in 2021. ACT Now has brought more than $100 million in sustainable investment to West Virginia. In 2023, President Brad Smith named him as Vice President for Workforce and Economic Development at Marshall University. As part of his role at Marshall, Brandon continues to lead the ACT Now Coalition.

He graduated from Shepherd University with a BA in history and holds a Master of Public Affairs from Indiana University. His PhD in human and community development is from West Virginia University. In 2017, Brandon was named West Virginian of the Year by *WV Living Magazine*. He is the winner of the JMK Social Innovation Prize, is a DRK Entrepreneur, and is an Ashoka Fellow. In 2019, Brandon was awarded the Heinz Award for Economy and Employment. For ten years, he has tried to learn the guitar but still knows only eight or nine songs (importantly, "Country Roads" is one of them).

Brandon, I've been looking forward to this. Your reputation precedes you. I'm thankful for Rohan Sandhu's introduction.

Yes, Rohan and I first connected through Brookings, and he was interested in a project I've been working on called the ACT Now Coalition. It has become a $100 million initiative for sustainable economic development in southern West Virginia.

Tell me about your background in West Virginia.

I go back on my dad's side in West Virginia. My mom's side goes back further than that in an area that used to be part of Virginia. My kids are either seventh or eighth generation; I never get it quite right. But there's a family farm in Braxton County where you see the headstones of multiple generations. I have a very deep sense of connection to this place.

Can you tell me about what sparked the creation of Coalfield Development fifteen years ago and what the organization does

today? I'm especially interested in how trust plays a role in Coalfield's work.

I loved growing up here, but like most young people who want to go to college, I assumed I would have to leave the area to find a good job. I went to Shepherd University and got involved with a Presbyterian church that was committed to social justice. Through that, I traveled quite a bit on service trips around the state and began to learn from those places.

I also saw that there was a lot of pain in those communities. Many of the challenges are generational in nature, so just parachuting in for a month or so was not enough time to make a big difference.

My last service trip was in the coal fields. We did home repair and other volunteer work. While we were there, two young men approached us and asked if we had any paid work. They literally had tool belts slung over their shoulders. I just couldn't shake the image. We have people who want to work, and they are wandering the streets with tool belts to find something to plug into.

I committed to starting a nonprofit to help. I went back to school to earn my master's degree and returned to West Virginia to start a social enterprise, Coalfield Development, serving southern West Virginia.

We hire crews to tear down abandoned houses, and we resell and reuse those materials. It is job creation and cultural development, eliminating eyesores for local people. Some of our crew members come from foster care or the penal system, and some are unemployed coal industry workers. Seeing what they can do with their own hands gives them purpose again and builds trust.

How important is trust building in your work?

Lack of trust is a deal breaker. It has to be tangible in a way that people can see it and experience it. Sometimes, it's experimental because we're in places that aren't necessarily thriving at the moment. We are willing to take risks.

We adopted some team principles to advance our work. And our top principles are trust and relationships. Trust is non-negotiable because projects will come and go—funding comes and goes; politicians come and go—but relationships outlive the projects. And relationships are what salvage projects when something goes wrong. If you haven't taken time to build trust, relationships can fall apart so quickly.

On a scale of one to ten, how would you rank the importance of trust in the work that you do?

An eight. Just because, when it comes to economic development, there is an element of luck involved.

Does trust boil down to individual relationships, or can it be embedded in the culture of a community?

Trust can totally be a part of the culture of a community. I'll try not to get too esoteric. Appalachia has a resource extraction history. And most of the money made off that process was outside the region, not inside the region. It was on the backs of the local people for the benefit of others.

But there's an underbelly to that story. It's easy to say robber barons came in and used us, but there are also local elites who benefited. They brought in wealthy interests and brokered the deals to get them the resources for very cheap and sometimes unethically. In many extractive communities, you see corruption. There are feudal-like setups with a few powerful families that own most of the businesses, land, and public offices. It isn't a culture that builds trust.

Do you think that feudal-like system is changing with new generations?

I'm hopeful. There's been an organic entrepreneurial movement in Appalachia. A lot of young people are saying, "We love this place, and our communities deserve better."

Let's talk about your strengths as a Trust Builder. Of the eight I listed, which ones speak to you?

Empathy and authenticity are two things for me. I was raised in a family of good storytellers and conversationalists. I feel like I can foster relationships through storytelling. I have genuine empathy, even with people with different belief systems from my own, by showing up reliably. Here, we've had the rug pulled out from underneath folks for a long time, and it can be hard to break through those promises being broken. So, you have to consistently show up and keep showing up.

It seems like West Virginia is a very relational state, versus transactional, when it comes to doing deals. Does that make trust-building harder or easier?

I think it's a little of both. I think it's harder at first if you're not from here. It can feel hard to break in. But one of the things that gives me hope is that when we do build trust, things move pretty quickly because it is a small state and a lot of people know each other.

What specific ways have you seen others in West Virginia build trust with each other?

There's no replacement for doing work. Together. When you're in the trenches together, side by side, that can build trust faster than anything. Show up, work hard, be competent. If I commit to doing something, it's crucial that I honor that. Fancy words and good stories only get you so far.

When has that ethic played a role in a big win for the state?

I'm thinking of the ACT Now Coalition. Our two largest cities, our two largest universities, for-profits, non-profits, and unions are all in the coalition together for a shared vision of economic diversification for twenty-one counties in southern West Virginia. We have consensus-based governance, so it moves a little slowly in that regard, but it's worth it because everybody's voice is heard. It's balanced. Instead of one university leading, they're co-equals. Same for Huntington and Charleston. As cities, they are equals at a table. The structure rewards a collaborative culture and transparency.

When we competed for a Build Back Better Regional Challenge grant, the Economic Development Administration (U.S. EDA) came back after the first round and said we needed to cut around 30 percent of the budget. There were eight different projects proposed in our application. For some communities, that could cause conflict: "Are you going to cut my project but not another?" Instead, we decided that everyone would equally cut 30 percent from their projects, and we would do so very transparently with each other. It wasn't easy, but it strengthened the coalition.

We were one of over six hundred applicants and one of the twenty-one winners. We received the third-largest award, $62.8 million, and we raised another $28 million in matching dollars.

Congratulations! I'm giving you a virtual high five.

Brandon, any parting words of wisdom?

The last thing I'll say for myself is, yes, I go way back in West Virginia, but I'm not a coal miner. My parents weren't coal miners. I think it's very important, too, to be authentic. I've only presented exactly who I am. I've not tried to be more or less than that. Sometimes, in community development, you might try to morph into someone else to do things faster. But in the long game, it's better to be yourself.

19
ADAM KNAPP

CEO, Leaders for a Better Louisiana

Baton Rouge, Louisiana

Trust Strengths

Empathy, Active listening

"Empathy is important to community development. It's critical to connecting with people and building relationships, and that is key to what economic developers do."

Adam is the chief executive officer of Leaders for a Better Louisiana and previously served as CEO of the Committee of 100 for Economic Development (C100). Prior to C100, Adam was president and CEO of the Baton Rouge Area Chamber, a regional economic development organization serving the nine-parish Capital Region of Louisiana.

Adam began his career in the private sector as a consultant for Accenture, a global consulting firm. A native of Lake Charles, Louisiana, Adam completed his bachelor's degree at Davidson College in North Carolina, studied in Germany, and attended executive programs at Harvard University's JFK School of Government.

Adam, thanks for joining me! My first question relates to the role of trust in economic development. On a scale of one to ten, how critical is it to creating a thriving community?

It's high. I feel like it's an eight or a nine.

I would give it a ten, but there's another factor at play. Trust only matters if local leaders care about economic development. I'm thinking specifically about elected officials with whom you need clear alignment to get a project done. If they don't prioritize economic growth, it really doesn't matter if you have trust.

I can see that, Adam. None of this matters if the people in charge don't think it's important.

Exactly.

I want to learn more about you and your style. I was fortunate to work with you on the Baton Rouge area's strategic plan, as well as some projects with your current organization. I've seen that you don't shy away from tough issues, but you do it in a way that's so approachable.

I've shared eight Trust Strengths and wonder which ones best describe you.

I spent a lot of time thinking about your list here, and it's a good list. Empathy and active listening are the ones that stand out the most. They're two sides of the same coin if you think about it. And those skills aren't easy to attain. When I work with folks who never built those muscles or lack those strengths, I see them struggling.

I totally agree. They could be seen as more "advanced" skills, if you will. Is it possible to teach people to be more empathetic or better listeners?

I think people have a strong capacity to fake empathy, but it's difficult to fake active listening. However, if someone has great listening skills, it can help them become more empathetic.

It might sound weird to say that empathy is important to community development. It's critical for connecting with people and building relationships, and that is key to what economic developers do.

Help me put it into context. Can you share an example?

It's like times when we've been in a room with a property owner, and we're trying to option their land for a future business site. Their first thought might be, *We don't want to hear from you. You're all shysters, and you won't offer me fair value for my land.*

Managing situations like that requires good listening and putting yourself in their shoes. You have to be present to earn their trust.

Here's another example. I see a lot of folks in our business pull out their laptops in meetings. They're taking notes, but it gives the impression that there is a thing between you and the person. It's not just younger people, either. If you're typing, you're not listening. How could you be actively listening and empathetic while you're on your laptop? Especially if the person is very much looking at you and engaging you, but your eyes are on the keyboard.

Oh, no, Adam. I'm typing right now as I interview you! I swear I'm listening, but now I'll close my laptop and rely on the recorded transcript. Does that feel better?

Haha! Yes!

Let's dive in a little deeper. What are other things you do to build trust with other leaders in Louisiana?

At the chamber, we led annual canvas trips in which local leaders visited another region for a few days. Yes, we learn about best practices while we're there, but these are actually corporate retreats. Companies take their leaders offsite to strategize about their business. Chamber-led leadership missions function in much the same way. We isolate time to think about the future of the community together. And we're convening people who would never otherwise have a chance to retreat together.

We haven't discussed this yet, but I feel like memory and recall are practices that build trust, too. I'm thinking of elected officials. If you remember what they care about and you follow up on it after the meeting, even months after, and even if it's a small thing, that small action goes a long way.

For example, recently, one of our biggest projects needed school board approval for a property tax exemption. I recalled something one of the board members cared about that had nothing to do with education or the project at hand. I asked him about it, and we had a great conversation. That person ended up voting in favor of the exemption because that moment of recall established trust between us.

Shifting gears, I want to ask you one of the questions that only a few others have answered. No pressure. Can you tell me about a shortcoming you've shared that helped build trust with others?

Just admitting that I made a mistake. To say, "I realize that was a crappy project, and I'm sorry I put you on the line. I'll find a better one and learn from this mistake." It can help recover a relationship and rebuild trust with others.

At work, this means that I admit to my staff that I tend to micromanage. In response, I've noticed that this gives them space to talk about their own shortcomings, and our relationship grows stronger.

You mentioned your team. What advice do you give them about building trust?

I tell them that it helps to have a structure for repetitive contact.

For example, the Baton Rouge area has nine counties. The region's success depends on the counties working together. So, when I led the chamber, we hosted a monthly get-together with the county and parish economic development people. The meetings started with a report on what they're working on, but ultimately, they turned into problem-solving sessions. They would share their challenges, and others would offer ideas, and that built rapport. Again, you need a regular cadence for them to gather over meals, coffee, or just coming to our office.

We mirrored that approach with other community leaders, especially when crises came up. We set a regular meeting time to convene leaders involved in the crisis.

I can't take credit for this, but my predecessor hosted a monthly dinner with just the mayor of Baton Rouge and the community foundation CEO. This happened every month for eight years! I continued the dinners when I stepped into the role. There's nothing like sharing a meal with someone.

At one point, we started talking about asking voters to approve funding for large-scale downtown revitalization, somewhere close to $1 billion. We invited other leaders to the dinners, donors started emerging, the mayor campaigned for it, and it got on the ballot. It was a massive bond. It didn't pass, but we only missed by four hundred votes. It wasn't the outcome we wanted, of course, but it shows that the trust built during those dinners encouraged the mayor to take a risk.

One last question, Adam. Other Trust Builders have discussed how a culture of trust among local leaders allows them to stretch out and take greater risks. How do you feel about that notion?

I've seen it. I don't think we could have landed an eight-hundred-job project with IBM if it weren't for the fact that the mayor was willing to take a risk with an upfront financial commitment. Because there was such strong trust with the mayor, he said yes to the ask and turned around an agreement letter within twenty-four hours. Since then, there have been fifteen years of tech jobs in downtown Baton Rouge. The risk paid off big time, but the risk may not have happened without trust. It's just awesome.

20

KIMM LAUTERBACH

President and CEO, REDI Cincinnati

Cincinnati, Ohio

Trust Strengths

Empathy, Transparency, Reliability

"We're doing this because we're motivated by something intangible. We're not just out there trying to have the best marketing campaign or the lowest cost. I want our region to be a better place for everyone. And the core of what we're doing is building trust."

As a founding member of REDI Cincinnati's leadership team, Kimm engineers strategies and tactics to strengthen the three-state, sixteen-county Cincinnati region's competitiveness globally. Kimm took the helm of REDI Cincinnati in September 2018, following five successful years as the organization's vice president of business development and project management. In that role, she helped change the face of economic development in the Cincinnati region, leading all aspects of deals for companies locating in or expanding within the region.

She has played a pivotal role in Ohio's economic development across multiple cities and counties, in both the public and private sectors, aligning diverse stakeholder interests with the needs of business communities to achieve long-term regional economic goals. Kimm serves on the boards of directors of the Cincinnati USA Regional Chamber and the Cincinnati Experience, as well as the Greater Cincinnati and Northern Kentucky Foreign Trade Zones, the BE NKY Growth Partnership, and the University of Cincinnati Research Institute.

Awards have highlighted Kimm's successful career, with the *Cincinnati Business Courier* naming Kimm its 2021 CEO of the Year for Small Nonprofit Organizations, which follows the publication's 2017 Women Who Mean Business recognition. In 2016 and again in 2021, Consultant Connect named her one of North America's Top 50 Economic Developers. Kimm is also recognized as a Woman of Influence by Venue and Lead Magazine and, in 2024, as a YWCA Career Woman of Achievement.

Kimm, we have known each other for almost ten years now, and we have worked together on two regional strategies as well as other projects. As we've discussed, and you've observed as well through your leadership in our field, sometimes communities that have every asset imaginable just can't get projects across the finish line. Do you think that trust among community leaders contributes to that dynamic?

I think that 95 percent of that is about trust. I've seen organizations that had a leader who was dynamic, but that person wasn't very trusted or had a reputation for being difficult. They were doing the work, but they weren't moving the needle.

You're getting into my next question. Can we talk about the eight Trust Strengths that I shared and talk about which ones are most "Kimm"?

I think, for me, it's empathy. I show up being incredibly empathetic. I listen that way. I don't have a great poker face because if something resonates with me, it resonates. If not, you can tell. If you compromise my trust, I have a very hard time coming back from that. I might trust to a fault.

When I started as president of REDI, I showed the community that my way is very open and transparent. For me, it's about leveraging our region's assets and not taking the credit.

Being willing to be empathetic and transparent is a risk. I don't think there is a secret sauce in what I do every day. Someone else could come in and do the tasks. But the difference is embracing the community and showing up in a genuine way versus coming in and thinking, *I'm the best, and you're lucky that I'm here.* With that attitude, nothing will move the conversation forward.

Kimm, when you think of someone who is new to their role or even new to a community, what stakeholder groups should be prioritized to build trust off the bat?

It depends on the organization, but if you're in a regional role, then it's about bridging relationships with local economic developers. Their realm is serving their local city or county, and they need to succeed within those borders. Trust building is so important to reassure them that you will support them and that they will continue to get the credit. I consistently show up and show that I'm standing strongly behind them and will help them no matter what. That's been a game-changer.

Several Trust Builders I've interviewed talked about the importance of not taking the credit. That must be difficult to do after you put so much effort into a project. How does that feel for your team?

It's frustrating sometimes, but at the end of the day, people know that we were hard at work even if we don't get the recognition. We use the Entrepreneurial Operating System as a team tool to clarify our vision and values. We talk a lot about our core values of being open and transparent and giving the best-in-class service. We touch back on those values when we reflect on project wins, reminding the team that we were the credible convener, and we provided the best service possible. Even if we don't get recognized for it, we know that was our win because we are adhering to our values.

It's ingrained in our culture to be humble. As long as we celebrate our internal successes, we don't have to be seen externally as the visible winner.

Also, we joke that there are very few true economic development crises. So we lost a project, or a deal went south? That stinks, especially when you're in the middle of it. But we aren't curing cancer. It's helpful to take the pressure off and be human.

I'd love to go into some specific things you do to build trust with others. Like, what would three o'clock on a Tuesday look like for you if it's not in the context of working on a giant project?

I have honest conversations with people about what I'm hearing. When our region was competing to keep the Cincinnati Open tennis tournament here and build a new facility, there were a lot of parties involved. We were in the middle, even though it wasn't clearly within our swim lane.

When I heard negative talk, I called one of the leaders involved and said, "I don't like what people are saying about you, and I think we should talk." Afterward, he and his team said it was one of the best calls they ever had because I had the courage to pick up the phone and be honest. It opened doors and helped keep the tournament here.

I have to ask since I am also a woman in the economic development field. Do you think there is a difference between the way a woman in a leadership position would handle a situation like that?

Oh, yes, for sure. I think the way that I show up every day is different. I've had people say to me, "You need to act like so-and-so, a man, in this situation." And I am like, "I'm still going to act like me."

I have to build a working relationship with our female and male leaders. I've been able to do that in a collaborative and non-threatening way, and that's served the Cincinnati region really well. And if a man showed up and had the same conversation in the same way, they might call him a name.

Ha! I won't quote you on that name, but I totally see your point.

Yes, and of course, I respect my male colleagues. We laugh that they could be a little more "Kimm" in situations and vice versa.

When you take a step back and look at how other leaders interact with each other, how are they building trust?

They consistently show up to collaborate. They share the credit with their partners. It's doing the work beforehand and socializing ideas, then sharing credit so that everyone feels like they have a role and are invested in a decision.

I have witnessed leadership structures of communities change over time. When I started my career, most places had a handful of leaders who seemed to be involved in everything. Today, it feels much more distributed. More voices might make it harder to get things done. How has this played out in the Cincinnati region?

For a long time, we had three major leaders. But now they are aging, and the next group is coming up. The original three did things because they passionately believed in and loved this region. Do the new leaders want the same thing? Probably, but we haven't seen it in action for as long a time. I think that communities that have figured out how to make that transfer have a higher level of trust.

REDI is one of only a handful of regional economic development organizations that covers three states. Does that complicate trust-building?

We have to figure it out and go to market together because it will ultimately benefit all three. Even if a project is located in one state, workers from other states get jobs. Policy-wise, I have been pushing for a formal partnership agreement, like the RED Zone concept, which has a joint tax-sharing agreement.

I want to lay the groundwork of trust daily so that when another giant opportunity, like a Tech Hubs grant or an Amazon HQ2, comes along, we aren't starting from scratch. I keep conversations going among leaders across borders so that we're ready.

Any parting words of wisdom?

We're doing this because we're motivated by something intangible. We're not just out there trying to have the best marketing campaign or the lowest cost. I want our region to be a better place for everyone. I'm not going to profit from it. The intrinsic motivation for doing these community-focused jobs is different, and the core of what we're doing is building trust.

21
KENNY MCDONALD

Founder, Little Dry Consulting

Columbus, Ohio

Trust Strengths

Integrity, Reliability

"You have to know that trust is paramount and that it can never be broken. You can make mistakes, but you can't break trust. Like here, we have to act regionally every single day. It's not an option to be regional only when it's convenient."

Kenny McDonald is an international thought leader in regional economic development. He has built and led teams in Columbus, Ohio; Charlotte, North Carolina; Albuquerque, New Mexico; and Savannah, Georgia. All of these organizations have been ranked in the top ten economic development organizations during his tenure.

McDonald also worked as a site location consultant for Fluor's Global Location Strategies practice, helping companies locate operations worldwide. He has served the economic development community as chairman of the International Economic Development Council and is a

Hall of Honor honoree in the Ohio Economic Development Association. He is the founder of Little Dry Consulting, which serves economic development organizations and provides location strategy for growing companies.

When I interviewed Kenny, he was president of OneColumbus, the regional economic development organization serving the 11-county Columbus, Ohio, region.

Kenny, I sent some questions in advance, but it's okay if this veers more conversational. First, I want to hear your thoughts on trust being a differentiator in economic and community development. If you rated it 1 to 10, where would it rank?

I think it's an eight or a nine. The only reason I would say eight is that, at some point, you're moving forward without trust. Someone has to take the first step. At some point, people just have to forge ahead with the work and believe that you're going to build trust because you do what you said you would do.

I was thinking about my first months up here. I had some strange meetings because they had tried to start a regional economic development organization before. There was some lack of trust, and some investors said they would withhold funding until they saw results. Eventually, they couldn't deny that we were delivering what we said we would. And it wasn't just about results. It was the way we were doing things. We were transparent.

We had to start with a coalition of the willing and then keep building. So, it takes a little leap of faith in these endeavors, whether it's workforce or economic development. Then you operate knowing that trust is paramount and that it can never be broken.

You can make mistakes, but you can't break trust. Like here, we act regionally every single day. It's not an option to be regional only when it's convenient. When we execute, it's consistent with our values.

You've mentioned a few things that built trust when you got there in 2010 to help stand up Columbus 2020. Can you tell me about a few of your strengths as a Trust Builder that helped back then?

Speaking about your values openly and then backing them up with correlated action so that they're one and the same. Your words and actions should be the same.

Part of it is surrounding yourself with people who are living up to those values and actions, too. Having people who are part of that ethos. It must be consistent from the board to the staff to the community. It has to be comprehensive.

I can't be in every room every day, so my team goes. And they operate with integrity, consistency, and transparency. They need to be respectful, too, because we're in front of groups with different viewpoints.

How do you help people find a common ground when they might be from different populations, geographies, or interest groups?

Start a question with "Couldn't we all agree that…?" It's like, "Couldn't we all agree that we want a great economy and jobs for our kids and grandkids? We all want to make this a better place. Do we agree that we need to adapt and grow?" Yes, 100 percent. Okay, let's start there and work backwards through the differences. It starts to diminish the differences and shows respect.

Let's talk about more detailed tactics.

I think vocabulary is a big deal. One, as the leader, the words you use and how you describe your work and mission should be consistent. That starts with your team. And then, when they go out and use that language consistently, people in the community hear that consistently and know that you're on the same page.

The other reason vocabulary is so critical in building trust is that you can measure it. You know you're making progress when other people use the same terminology. Pretty soon, it becomes common vernacular. People might not always agree, but at the same time, they're using our words. Count that as a win.

Do you do anything with your team, like starting every meeting with the same repeat of values or mission? Any rituals that reinforce the consistency you're talking about?

Yes. We start with the vision, even in normal meetings. I did that this morning with a group of smaller communities. I started by saying, "The bigger idea is that we think this region can do something really special." It anchors you in what you're about to say in the rest of the presentation, and it reminds people that we're trying to do something larger than whatever the meeting is about.

The key with a vision is to repeat it, repeat it, repeat it until it becomes vocabulary. Everybody likes to pursue things that are bigger than themselves. Even the people with the most selfish interests want that. They'll come to meetings with a personal agenda, and starting off with vision is a good way to help everyone take a deep breath.

End the meeting with it, too, like, "Couldn't we all agree that if we did some of this stuff, we would be taking a step forward?" Around the time you get sick of saying it, they are starting to adopt it.

I've always admired the camaraderie in your region among local economic developers, the "LEDOs." I don't see that as much in other regions. Is there anything special you do to help that group trust each other?

One is spending time together. It's hard not to trust or have empathy for people that you spend a lot of time with. You're going to find out things about them, their common challenges, and things like that. For the past fifteen years, we've gathered them every month in a room for a few hours to talk about regional issues.

It's also a way to assimilate new people coming into the region. They can feel comfortable and that they aren't alone. There's a cohort here who has their back and can show them the ropes.

Whenever you have time to go away from home with someone, you break down other barriers. We host annual retreats with the LEDOs. We do that intentionally because we know that if there is trust among them, then good things will happen. Or, if someone makes a mistake, we can say, "We know they are a good person, so let's reach out to solve that together."

Like you, another interviewee talked about building a culture where mistakes can be made. She also talked about how people in this community development profession don't always get the credit for progress.

Community leaders have to be wired differently. Take pride in not being out in front. Everyone you're interviewing for this book probably has that mentality. It's professional practice to put everyone else out in front. It's not because we're gracious; it's because it's part of the job. It ties back to the values we talked about. If people embrace our values, then not being on stage is easier for them.

I want to roll down into a few more specifics. Are there things you've observed other community leaders doing to build trust?

To advance a community, you need allies that share a purpose with you. They're willing to do some things even against their own interests in the short term to gain a long-term win for the region. Even if we miss, we'll learn from that and come back stronger.

In today's age, is it getting more difficult to build trust with other local leaders?

No, not with each other as individuals. I think what's changed is trust in institutions. Selling to the public has become harder because institutional trust is eroding. Doing things that involve public processes, like zoning changes or whatever, to get a project done is now slower. That's why you need to share the vision broadly with diverse public groups and speak to people who wouldn't traditionally want to hear from you, including the media. You say, "This is a step toward our vision of greater prosperity. This is the 'greater good' and part of our long view." If we don't tell them, it can be hard for political people to say that.

I agree. People in our profession, community and economic developers, have a pulpit to share that message and gain buy-in that politicians may not have.

Trust is built when people go do something together. If you're waiting until trust is built and everything is in perfect shape before you take action, then you'll lose out. Instead, trust grows when people work on a hard, common initiative and eat pizza at the office late at night, forming bonds. The *work* of the work leads to building trust.

Kenny, final question. If you were asked by another community to come in and start up a new Columbus 2020-like organization, would you do things differently?

I would try to bring the same energy. But I would do it with a little more patience to bring people along. I've been through enough battles that I have more patience today. I wouldn't get as fired up about folks who put their personal agendas first and are passively against you.

Any last words of wisdom for this book?

Every community has people of good intentions, but fewer people with good intentions who are also willing to pay the price to build trust over the long term. I do agree with your theory that higher-performing communities have higher levels of trust. Everyone can be successful with some good luck, but you're going to miss opportunities or not even recognize them unless there is a culture of trust.

22

RON KESSLER

The Kessler Group

Austin, Texas

Trust Strengths

Integrity, Authenticity, Active Listening

"Putting yourself out there is important. Isolation is anti-trust, anti-social, anti-other. If you isolate yourself, you don't know much about others. You have to be comfortable with the mystery, innuendo. Not everything is black and white."

Following a thirty-five-year career as a lawyer, Ron created the Ron Kessler Group to provide one-on-one executive and leadership coaching to help clients achieve greater performance and profitability. Ron focuses his leadership and coaching experience on people and enterprises seeking to maximize their full potential through values-based personal and professional growth, productivity, and profits. RKG's vision statement is "to build leaders, one champion at a time." He was shaped by his legacy of leadership roles in community service, law firms, and the church.

Ron is passionate about regional and entrepreneurial economies and has served universities, chambers, and the private sector in creating entrepreneurial networks that commercialize technology, create jobs and wealth, and grow and retain indigenous enterprises. He is a former partner-in-charge of the Austin office of Jones Day and a former partner at Troutman Pepper Locke.

He was the 1993 Chair of the Austin Chamber of Commerce, a past president of the Austin Area Research Organization, and a present board member. Ron also serves on the advisory board of Frost Bank/Austin and has served on the advisory boards of the Nature Conservancy of Texas, IC2, and the Center for American and International Law. He was the first chair of Advantage Austin, a member of the board of Seton Cove, and a co-founder of the Conservation Luncheon of the Texas Nature Conservancy.

In 2014, Ron received the Father of the Year Award from the American Diabetes Association. He is also a former board member of the Texas Civil Justice League; the Advisory Council of the University of Texas, College of Fine Arts; board member of Rites of Passage Development, Inc. (Greater Calvary Bible Church); and an adjunct professor at the Episcopal Seminary of the Southwest.

In Dallas, he was elected Dallas County Democratic Chair (1976 and 1978), was a candidate for the Texas State Senate (1980, 16th District), and served as chair of the Dallas Legal Services Foundation, Inc.

Born in Dodge City, Kansas, and raised in Hutchinson, Kansas, he attended the University of Kansas and came to Texas in 1963 to attend law school at SMU. After graduating in 1966, he served in the Peace Corps in Venezuela. He and Vicki were married in Caracas and returned to Dallas in 1968 to start their family and Ron's legal career. They are proud parents of Kristin Schell, Matt Kessler, and Emily Carter and have nine grandchildren. They have lived in Austin since 1987.

Ron, you've been a dear friend and coach for more than a decade. Since the early years of my career, I have been inspired by your lead-

ership as one of the architects of Austin's unmatched success in economic development.

We've talked about trust a lot through the years. On a scale of one to ten, to what degree does trust among community leaders contribute to a community's prosperity?

I would give it a nine or ten. It's very important. I don't think much can get done without trust. People walk away from folks who aren't trustworthy. They may continue to work, but they won't give their best. The alternative is that others will look past issues and do the work if it's someone they trust.

Do you think that trust sparks people to act even if a full plan isn't in place yet?

Yes, in a trusting culture, I think people will continue to give their best even if they may not see how it fits into the outcome, particularly if there's not a plan in place. It's a much better outcome because they trust the leader to find the plan.

You've had so many different leadership roles in your life, Ron. I can't even begin to list them all and the impact that you've had on Austin's growth. But I want to know more about your personal trust-building strengths.

I like the list of eight Trust Strengths that you sent.

The law firm I was in charge of, my civic activities where I was active and even ran for public office, and the role I played in building the technology economy here, and ultimately moving into leadership coaching.

I was a coach in the law firm well before I started coaching as a business. I learned that the leader wasn't necessarily the smartest person in the room. People tend to follow somebody who can bring others together for a common purpose. To do that, there has to be a high degree of trust.

So, is one of your strengths convening people?

Right. And in the law practice as a partner, I helped other lawyers. They might not have the network that I did. Strengthening others is critical. I think focusing on building up another person is a strong leadership trait. It results in trust. In Austin, I met a lot of people who were in their prime, the best in the world at what they did, like the University of Texas' engineering dean, business school dean, or president.

And it took someone like Pike Powers to knit them all together. He had a way of getting people to work together to see a common vision. There was perseverance and not allowing somebody's "no" to be their final answer.

I was lucky to know Pike and attend some of his dinners. He would bring together people who might not know each other, but he engaged them around his idea. Sometimes, you didn't know where it was going, but you were honored to be there because you trusted Pike. And I always said yes to his dinner invitations. I miss him.

Do you have anything else to share on the Trust Strengths? I bet you have more.

The point about integrity intrigues me. There is an ethical component to trust building. Someone might make an ethical mistake and get by with it, but someone who is totally unethical, lies, and is self-centered can hang in there for a while, but they're not long-term.

We've been dancing around it, but can you share specific things you have done to build trust with other community leaders?

Listening is an important factor of trust. Being open to biases you might have. Be very honest and say that you're not comfortable.

Can you share more techniques around active listening?

Are there people whom I've listened to or should have listened to in my life? Are there still some today? I have a friend whom I've known for forty years with a different faith from mine. I like to hear his perspective. Another school friend is a retired doctor, and I talk to him on the phone every two weeks. These conversations are different from my usual ones, and it makes me listen from a different perspective than I would otherwise.

I think putting yourself out there is important. Isolation is anti-trust, anti-social, anti-other. If you isolate yourself, you don't know much about the others. You have to be comfortable with the mystery, innuendo. Not everything is black and white.

Some people have a hard time with the gray area.

You're right. Being out there, keeping an open mind, and staying curious are important ingredients for Trust Builders.

My poetry helps me with that. I read poems, I write poems, and I see things I wouldn't have ever seen through that. A poem might mean something different to you than it does to me. My experiences are different, and our minds have been wound and wired. We have to appreciate that. People who trust others and are trusted tend to have a flow that allows other perspectives to enter.

You're bringing up a tough topic, which is that isolation is an epidemic in our country. Do you think that building trust is more challenging because of that?

Yes, it's harder because of the isolation and social media. Social media confuses the whole issue of ethics: right and wrong. People tend to believe the last thing that they saw on social media.

I would love to share stories of times when trust has helped a community's opportunity come to fruition. Can you think of an example, a story?

Sometimes, it's a win that resulted and wasn't predicted. That's because you had a plan and a goal, and you had the right pieces in place. Then something came along later, and those pieces played into a totally different outcome than the plan.

For instance, the semiconductor fabs in Austin. They were built to bring capacity within the U.S. for companies that need that kind of technology. And then along comes Tesla, in part because of the region's strength in semiconductors and technology. Regional leaders had already done the hard work and were able to win that investment because of something they prepared well beforehand.

Before we leave, can you offer me any advice for this book?

You need to *do* this book.

I want to leave you with a poem called "Motto" by David Berman. It says:

"I want to be famous so that I can be humble about being famous.

What good is humility when I am stuck in this obscurity?"

Thank you for sharing, Ron. I don't know about being famous, but I appreciate the challenge of sharing my ideas and seeing where it goes. I value our friendship so much, and your wisdom has been a game-changer in my life.

23

CHARLES WOOD

President and CEO, Chattanooga Area Chamber of Commerce

Chattanooga, Tennessee

Trust Strengths

Integrity, Reliability, Competency

"You can get some things done without trust. You can operate in a more transactional way, and people will do it because it's good for their personal agendas. But moving really big, complicated initiatives forward is very hard to do without trust."

Charles Wood serves as CEO for the Chattanooga Area Chamber of Commerce and previously served as the chamber's vice president of economic development. Prior to joining the Chattanooga Chamber, Charles held economic development positions at chambers of commerce in Pensacola, Florida, and Mobile, Alabama, and worked in local government in Texas.

During his more than twenty-five-year career, Charles has led marketing, recruitment, and expansion efforts that have created thousands of jobs across dozens of companies, including Hewlett-Packard, Mellon Financial, and Volkswagen.

Charles holds a master's degree in economic development from the University of Southern Mississippi and holds the designation of Certified Economic Developer (CEcD) from the International Economic Development Council.

Charles and his wife, Angie, have one grown son and live in downtown Chattanooga. In his spare time, he crews on sailboats, cooks Cajun food, and can be found at his son's coffee shop on the Northshore in Chattanooga.

I've been thinking about the topic of trust and economic development for many years. Last year, I found some time to start exploring in depth.

I think it's an awesome idea. It's a growing concern on multiple levels, from local to national. So much boils down to trust. In the community-development world, it's critical to making sure you can get things done.

It seems like the concept of working with a mindset of abundance is fading. There is a dynamic of needing to protect what we have. Don't grow too fast. There are concerns about resources. And when you look at conversations around those things, trust plays a big role.

What's behind, as you put it, the fading mindset of abundance?

If you think about Chattanooga's history, in the 1980s, we started the process of reinvigorating our downtown. There was a lot of community input. We have a legacy of bringing people together, inviting people in, and building trust by doing that. There is still strong trust among other institutions, like our nonprofits. But we're seeing some of that dynamic shifting on the political side, especially around growth versus anti-growth.

That's something that I've heard from other interviewees. They point to an era when people came together around a big project, like downtown, riverfront, or broadband in Chattanooga. Those initia-

tives were so successful that they established an expectation of setting aside differences and working together. Is that spirit fading?

It's still happening in many ways.

I'd like to get into some specifics. But first, on a scale of one to ten, how important is trust in community and economic development?

I put it at an eight. You can get some things done without it. You can operate in a more transactional way, and people will do it because it's good for their personal agendas. But moving big, complicated initiatives forward consistently is very hard to do without trust.

Transactional versus relational communities. I've been noodling on how those two ways of operating impact trust and progress. Thanks for bringing that up.

We are very much a relationship-oriented economy. I think that tone is set by leaders. But it can also bubble up.

Another question is about your own trust-building strengths. What do you think of the list of eight Trust Strengths that I sent to you?

To me, integrity is a baseline. It's foundational. And showing up reliably and consistently is key. I've been in Chattanooga for a long time. That's been a big part of how I've operated. And then competency and credibility.

I didn't grow up in a traditional environment. For a long time, I didn't share that. I'm around people who are pretty well-off. So, I used to tamp down. It's only been in the last five years that I've been more comfortable sharing my background. It's easy to put on a professional façade and try to have people think you're like them. And so, authenticity is something to work on.

Showing up consistently and reliably are strengths that I've seen in you. I remember you met with more than a hundred people after we finished the first Chattanooga Climbs strategy. I don't have many other clients who personally led that level of outreach.

That's what I do: lots of one-on-one meetings wherever they are, not in my office. That matters.

Can you share some specific tactics, Charles? We started talking about politics when we kicked off. How are you bridging the divide?

We started hosting joint city council and county commission meetings. We bring our eleven county commissioners and nine city council members together to talk about one big topic. Our goal is to do that twice a year. Sometimes, the topic just pops up because it's problematic. Sometimes, it's more intentional and strategic. Either way, it's meant to get them off the dais and together.

We even seat city council members next to county commissioners whose districts overlap. Then, after those sessions, we have some food together and hang out so that they can get to know each other.

Assuming those meetings are posted and public, do people from the general public show up?

It depends on the topic. Sometimes, only a few. We did one around the new AA baseball stadium, and it was standing room only. We probably had seventy people in the audience, news cameras, all that kind of stuff.

I look forward to seeing a game in the new stadium. I'm sure trust played a big role in moving that project forward.

It's on an old foundry site that was a visible brownfield when you drove in from Nashville. The master developer cut his teeth as project manager on Ponce City Market in Atlanta and is just finishing up the Neuhoff District redevelopment in Nashville. We are incorporating all those old foundry buildings into the stadium. I have been told, under no uncertain circumstances, that this will be the coolest AA baseball stadium in the country.

A home run! Literally.

Is there anything specific you do to get in front of the anti-growth contingency?

We're starting a campaign that's basically the face of economic development. We want to spotlight individuals who have been directly impacted in a positive way by the economic development work we've done. That can be an ex-offender who is now employed or an entrepreneur we've supported. The goal will be to showcase stories on a very personal level.

It's a little tricky because some people don't want visibility. They're nervous about social media backlash and stuff like that.

We're also working on leveraging our young professionals group. We're trying to start a chapter of YIMBYs, "Yes In My Backyard," making the point that they want more opportunity, housing options, dating options, etc.

And any practical recommendations on how to handle a situation when most of the community supports a project, but one or two powerful local leaders stand in the way?

Take all measures to ensure they don't look wrong.

You know, several years ago, the county mayor and the city mayor didn't see eye to eye. They were in different political parties. In public, however, they appeared together and supportive of each other. They behaved like statesmen. Encourage that in others.

That's good advice in life, too.

Okay, one final question. Charles, can you tell me about a time when trust among local leaders helped move a big project forward?

The stadium project was one. Another happened during COVID. We weren't involved in it, but other local partners were. We have a pretty sizable population that is low-income. When we sent kids home during the pandemic, our partners started a program called EdConnect. It was a collaboration between EPB, our electric power provider, which also has fiber, and the Enterprise Center, which is a group that does a lot of outreach around digital equity. The city and county were funding partners. The program rolled out free high-speed broadband to all households with kids who qualified for free or reduced lunch in Hamilton County schools. EdConnect is still going today.

I know that the chamber and business community in Chattanooga is doubling down on its commitment to K-12 education, and it's inspiring. I look forward to watching your progress!

24

CHRIS FRASER

Principal and Regional Managing Director, Avison Young

Greenville and Charleston, South Carolina

Trust Strengths

Integrity, Respecting differences

"When we win, it's because everybody is at the table and no one is fighting to take credit. We all get the spotlight instead of individually pushing to the podium."

As managing director of Avison Young's South Region, comprising offices across North and South Carolina, Georgia, Tennessee, and Florida, Chris plays a pivotal leadership role in shaping the firm's regional strategy. His deep understanding of market dynamics and close connection to regional trends and information give him the perspective needed to advise colleagues and clients on industry activity and emerging opportunities. He is a passionate leader and problem solver committed to empowering others to succeed and driving success across the organization.

Chris is also a market leader in the Charleston, Greenville, and Savannah markets and is heavily involved in the community, having served in volunteer leadership roles across these markets, including education, the arts, and economic development.

Most recently, Chris was chair of the Charleston Regional Development Alliance, a tri-county economic development agency for the Charleston, South Carolina, region. He is a current member of the Palmetto Beacon Venture Fellowship, focused on developing the life science cluster in the region.

Chris, first, I thoroughly enjoyed working with you on the Charleston region's recent innovation-led strategy as well as past plans. You've served on the boards of and chaired numerous economic, education, and community development organizations within your region and state. I can't wait to hear your perspectives on local trust building.

To start, on a scale of one to ten, to what degree does trust among community leaders contribute to success in economic development?

It's up there, a nine or a ten. Everyone needs to trust the people they work with and trust that everybody's aligned around what needs to happen. The converse of that is when people have personal agendas that don't line up. Then you get at odds. If you don't have trust, you don't have anything. In the absence of trust, you simply won't be successful long term.

Think about growing a region's economy. Whether a company is located on the right side or the left side of a geopolitical line on a map, it's irrelevant. People live, work, and spend money everywhere. So, you want to be in a place where people trust each other across lines, and everybody says, "Hey! They win, we win."

It's interesting that you jumped up to the regional level. I haven't defined the geographic borders of "local trust" as I'm exploring in this book. How far out can you go and effectively, consistently build trust? Block by block? At the city or county level? A metro region

with multiple counties? What comes to mind when you think about this concept in practice?

It's whatever someone's scope of influence is. You need to build trust within that space. My work and volunteer positions span several regions in South Carolina, and I need to have trusting relationships in all of them.

I'd like to focus on your strengths as a Trust Builder based on the eight Trust Strengths that I'm exploring. I've seen you in action through my work in Charleston and have my own guesses. I'm very curious. Are there one or two that resonate as being unique to your style?

I think you need them all. I'm big on doing the right thing. Having integrity. Reputations take a long time to get established, and they can be destroyed in minutes.

The second one that spoke to me is respecting others' differences. I try to allow people to feel heard and respected. We don't have to agree with each other. Those open conversations, even when people don't see eye to eye, are critical to progress and very important to building trust.

Let's talk about integrity. It's such an essential part of building trust. What do you do specifically that reinforces your integrity?

I'm in the commercial real estate business, and I've always taken the position that my clients' interests come first. If you're in it for the long haul, you must be able to say, "Hey, I know you're looking at this property. I don't advise you to buy it, and here's why." That costs me money at the moment. If I wanted to sell it to you without any thought of responsibility for what happens, my integrity would be at risk, and I would break trust. That's a big price to pay in the long run.

I use that as a lens, even with my junior colleagues. If you're going to be in this business for twenty or thirty years, having integrity in every deal matters.

I love the long-game perspective, Chris. It seems like being "in it to win it" would make someone more inclined to foster trust with others. Then again, unfortunately, that's not always the case.

I've been thinking about the mechanics of how to ramp up when a new project comes along. Say it's a potential new business investment or a new community program that requires multiple organizations to be involved. How do you determine who to include in the first round of conversations and then grow the circle as the opportunity progresses?

I start with the people who are going to be affected, whether positively or negatively, making sure that those folks are aware of what's going on. I have one-to-one meetings with them, first to say what we're trying to accomplish and then listen to their concerns. It might take more time in the beginning, but it saves time in the end.

Ideally, yes, but what if you simply don't have time? What role does trust play when there is an accelerated timeline?

Having an existing foundation of trust is critical. Otherwise, it might feel like people falling out of a plane without parachutes. You've got to trust that people will do the things they're supposed to do in the right way. That culture of trust is developed over time, not during a situation.

Speaking of building a culture of trust, what specific things do you or others in the region do to foster that?

For me, it's the fact that I've done it for so long and been consistent. I've always had a view that I need to give back to my community, however I can, to make an impact. It's one thing for somebody to drop in on an opportunity and pull out when it's over. It happens. It's fine. But it doesn't contribute to creating a culture of trust. Consistent commitment does. Showing up and dedicating personal time for the good of the community over individual motives. Leaders must also pass that along to younger generations.

It's not always easy for a young person to say, "This thing I'm doing,

if I keep doing it for thirty years, I'll be a better local leader because people will trust me." What advice do you have?

Start with today. Just get involved! There's so much work to be done in any community. Surely, there is something they feel strongly about right now. This is relationship work. I challenge future generations to get involved and stay involved in something they care about.

I like the positivity, Chris! Drilling down a little more, how can a business encourage its younger employees to do this? After all, work may be an excuse not to be civically involved.

My firm has a chamber of commerce membership. I tell our team that they have access to all chamber activities and networking. We will also sponsor certain things, but they've got to get out and be visible. Have integrity and a moral compass. It will happen over time. They might get bruised along the way, but keep it up.

What about people who are new to the community? How do you bring them into the fold so that they can form real, trustful relationships?

We have entities in Charleston, like the Regional Development Alliance, the chamber, and others, who are the voices of the region. When new execs move into the market, they get assimilated into these organizations. Because our culture of trust is pervasive and long-term, they tend to pick up on the culture, and the walls come down because we've created a safe space. They realize this isn't a place where everyone is trying to get into their pocket. A trustful culture transcends transactional mindsets.

When we win, it's because everybody is at the table and no one is fighting to take credit. We all get the spotlight instead of individually pushing to the podium.

Economic development is a team sport, and it doesn't work if the team members don't trust each other.

That's right. If everyone is out for the right reasons, then everyone shares in the success.

25
DAVID GINN

President and CEO, Charleston Regional Development Alliance

Charleston, South Carolina

Trust Strengths

Reliability, Authenticity

"To me, the most foundational way for leaders to trust each other is by having a well-researched, regional economic development strategy that is professionally developed, written, and shared among the community."

David has been with the CRDA since its inception, serving as the organization's executive vice president and project director before being named president and CEO in 2000. A Certified Economic Development Professional, he maintains a comprehensive awareness of current issues in economic development, thanks in part to affiliations with the International Economic Development Council and as past president of the S.C. Economic Developers Association. He has also held professional economic development and industrial marketing positions in Atlanta and Savannah.

David grew up in the Atlanta area and holds a degree in economics and international business from the University of Southern Mississippi. He also studied abroad at the London School of Economics. He and his wife, Jean, live in Mount Pleasant, and they have two adult children and one daughter-in-law.

David, I've personally seen you in action as a Trust Builder in the Charleston region for more than twenty years now, and you've been with the CRDA for longer than that. I'd love to hear from you. On a scale of one to ten, to what degree does trust among community leaders contribute to success in economic development?

For me, relationships are the most important aspects of life: first, my relationship with God, then my wife, children, family, friends, and colleagues. However, I also know and believe that trust is at the core of each of those healthy relationships, in all its varieties. Therefore, on a scale of one to ten, I would rank trust as a ten, the most critical factor.

What Trust Strengths best describe you as a Trust Builder? I shared eight with you. Which ones are most like David?

In my view, trusting someone involves a willingness to be vulnerable, despite uncertainty, because you have a positive expectation of their actions. Being authentic, consistent, and honest allows for the strongest form of trust to build between two people. Therefore, the two traits you've mentioned that meet most of my thoughts are reliability and authenticity.

Those make sense to me, too, David. I've seen you at work, and I have always appreciated your willingness to be there, open up to people, and do so in a way that is humble and humorous. I doubt you would say that about yourself because you are just that— humble, but I'm allowed to say it.

I appreciate that, Amy.

I'd like to drill down to specifics so that readers can learn tactics. What specific things do you do to build trust with other community leaders?

One of the best things we do as a regional economic development alliance is to regularly bring our three county economic development partners together with our business development team and share all the new, active, and developing project details with each other. By sharing all the project activity every couple of weeks and then growing that confidential, regional economic development team to include our energy providers, port, rail, and training partners, we send a strong message that we're all in this very competitive landscape together.

Ultimately, when a prospect comes to the region, it's clear to them that the team not only know each other, but they have also prepared in advance. These meetings have been operating for years, and the trust level is high. The frustration about not knowing what's going on in the market is relatively low.

One other important ally we include, once the project parameters are known, is calling the state's business development team and asking that a project manager be assigned to work with our regional point of contact. This allows for a prospect to feel a seamless partnering and have a trusting team they can rely on during their search process and beyond.

I've participated in those meetings through my consulting work, and I can testify that regularly scheduled meetings with county leaders and others have outsized benefits. I know you and your team initiate those. Are there things that you observe other community leaders doing to foster trust with each other?

To me, the most foundational way for leaders to trust each other is by having a well-researched, regional economic development strategy that is professionally developed, written, and shared among the community. It's important that each leader, no matter their background, has a mutual foundation or beginning point to begin understanding the region's strengths and weaknesses, how and where we can compete, and then their conversation potentially can move to a more trusting conversation or relationship over time, since they've already agreed on a number of basics.

At that point, they can use their business experience, elected-leader experience, or academic leadership background to begin solving the challenges and goals set forth in the strategic vision and plan. When nothing exists to align around, confusion, mistrust, frustration, and lack of winning all begin to erode trust and can take communities down an unhealthy road.

Given my background as a strategist, I especially love that answer. I've been a facilitator in four of the last five CRDA-sponsored five-year strategies, starting in 2004. I have seen your region's leaders coalesce around strategy. They all deserve high fives for committing to plans because the results there have been phenomenal.

I've been fortunate to meet a lot of your region's leaders, but I'm curious about your experience. Can you tell me about a community leader you deeply trust?

For me, having many mentors along my life's journey has made my life possible. Beginning with my parents, then aunts and uncles stepping in, wise businessmen, a spiritual director, Bible study leaders, radical mentoring, and professional coaches.

However, one community leader who has had, and still has, my best interest in his heart is Bill Finn, retired chairman and CEO of AstenJohnson, a global manufacturer of industrial felts that are used in the paper-making process. Their international headquarters is here in North Charleston. So, in addition to being a top business executive for most of his career, he also volunteered at one time as chairman of the CRDA.

Through a mutual friend, Bill arranged for me to meet him in Hilton Head for lunch one Sunday. This was in 1992, when I was vice president with the Savannah Economic Development Authority. Following that meeting, I was hired to lead regional economic development in Charleston, beginning in April of 1993, and Bill has been coaching me up ever since that moment in time. I will always be eternally grateful for his support, trust, friendship, guidance, and consistent advice over the past thirty-two years.

That story is so inspirational—more than thirty years of mentorship. Can we pledge right now that we will pass that forward and be mentors to others? If you were mentoring someone right now who wants to improve their ability to build trust with others, what advice would you give them?

Showing up when possible seems to be a large percentage of the success matrix. Be authentic and focused on the person in front of you, avoid or politely step away from gossip-related conversations, and, when mistakes are made, be quick to admit it, apologize sincerely, and then move forward. Over time, these honest and authentic approaches to people and relationships build trust, which in turn allows you to build meaningful and productive relationships.

I love this! In Austin, we used to say, "Show up, be positive, and stay above the line." It sounds like a football coach, but it applies to trust building as well.

I don't want to end on a sour note, but you have a story to tell related to trust that will be really helpful to other community leaders. I observed this from afar and saw you and your partners work hard to restrengthen trust very successfully. I know it couldn't have been easy. Can you tell me about that time, a decade or so ago, when diminishing trust caused a challenge for your region?

Happy to share that story, Amy, because there are lessons that could be helpful to others. And we came out stronger on the other end.

Over a dozen years ago, our public-private partnership focused on regional economic development was in jeopardy due to several issues. For a variety of reasons, the public-sector leaders felt left out of our regional process and leadership opportunities. In fact, our bylaws only allowed them to appoint representatives to our board, but not actually serve themselves.

With this lack of trust and engagement, the public-sector leaders decided they wanted to create a new and duplicative regional economic development model with only public-sector leaders. In effect, this would have left our region with two competing entities within the same three-county region, both with the same mission.

After two years of working through these trust, control, and credit issues, the top business leaders, in conjunction with our state's secretary of commerce, agreed in part with the elected leaders. By acknowledging that I could easily be replaced, the business model we were operating under could also certainly be adjusted or changed.

But the business leaders also concluded that they would fall on their swords in support of having only one public-private partnership for economic development in the Charleston region. That strong stand, plus agreements to change the bylaws and elevate the top county and city elected leaders to the regional board and executive committee, all allowed for trust to be restored. It's somewhat odd how quickly things moved to a healthy place throughout the region. And today, the trust, peace, and leadership for regional economic development are stronger now than ever before.

That's a high note I love to hear. Thank you, David! As you said, sometimes, the most challenging times can elevate a region in the long run when leaders are committed to the best for their community. If that common thread exists, love for a place beyond personal gain, a tough time has the potential to lay a stronger foundation than ever experienced before.

26

ED GARDNER

Vice President, Business and Economic Development, Entergy Mississippi, LLC

Jackson, Mississippi

Trust Strengths

Reliability, Authenticity, Competency

"I've always tried to meet people where they are, no matter what it's for. I think that's important. It breaks down barriers and builds trust. I'll drive two hours for lunch just to show someone that I care. It shows people respect."

Ed is responsible for fostering economic growth in Entergy Mississippi's service territory through collaborative business development efforts with state and local allies. Gardner has been instrumental in both business expansion and new business development, including helping to secure Amazon Web Services' historic $10 billion investment in the state.

Prior to joining Entergy in 2015, Ed was with PowerSouth Energy Cooperative, providing economic development services to Northwest

Florida. Other experience includes positions in Birmingham, Alabama, and Auburn, Alabama. He is a Certified Economic Developer and a Certified Economic Development Finance Professional.

Hi, Ed! To start, I have a premise that trust among local leaders is the most important aspect of economic development. Does that make sense to you? Could you rank it on a one-to-ten scale?

I think it's super important. I doubt many people would say that it's a two. I would place it as an eight or nine.

Some people think that economic developers are just salespeople. To me, the best economic developers are not salespeople. In fact, I think the worst ones are. I don't even like using salesy superlatives like "the best," "unmatched," or "unparalleled" because it's probably not true. To me, everything we do is about being truthful, and that builds trust. It's not just a matter of being right or wrong. It's about being credible.

I'm curious. As a person in a statewide role covering forty-five counties, how do you coach local leaders if they don't have much experience working together?

We've structured it. We worked with a few consultants who developed Delta team training. It would include the local economic developer and then five or six other local leaders who would be involved in a site visit.

Right. Companies and site consultants considering a community for expansion can sense whether those leaders trust each other. Training in advance is helpful.

When we get a new economic developer that comes into our territory and shows a lot of promise, more than anything, a willingness to work with others, we try to jump in as quickly as possible to help them. We'll offer site-visit training, helping their board understand the community's challenges and opportunities. I really look for local leaders who are actually interested in getting help. Some don't want it, and that's okay, too.

Can you see a correlation between economic growth in the counties that ask for help and those that don't?

I can't say whether they're winning more deals or not, but they are absolutely succeeding. There are only a few communities here that win what most consider to be significant deals, like a major company locating in their county. A lot of the time, the real wins are getting a new infrastructure project, or success at their college, or a program that helps existing businesses.

Again, they have to be open to receiving our help. I am thinking of a relatively new economic developer here in Mississippi who is fantastic. She sees Entergy as a resource and access to the higher-end offerings we provide. We've given her grants and helped her get a qualified industrial site in the Mississippi Delta, one of the few in the Delta. Hopefully, they will land a project one day. Because they ask for help, I know they'll win community support to do big things.

That is important to say: success in local communities isn't always about landing a five-hundred-employee company. It can be about a new educational program or even just reversing population loss.

You're interacting with a large constituency, Ed. What are some of the skills you use to build trust with all those local leaders?

I think authenticity is my first one. Like, if you see me out and about, I'm usually in my favorite trail-running shoes and my best Grateful Dead t-shirt, and I just don't care. I'm happy about that.

I also think it's competency. I really like helping other people. For example, if I hear about a great job opening, I tell my staff, even if it's one of my best people. I don't want to hold them back. And I'll preface it with, "I don't want you to go anywhere, but there's this opportunity."

I would get a little paranoid if my boss kept sharing job openings with me.

Haha! Even if someone gets a better opportunity, that's really good for us because we'll always be able to attract top talent if we help people reach their highest potential.

Authenticity and competency are totally you, Ed. I can see that. Can you share a specific tactic that you use to build trust?

One little thing that I learned a long time ago, and I don't know if it's because I like to travel, but I don't like my office. At all. I joke with people that everybody can use my office because I am rarely there.

I've always tried to meet people where they are, no matter what it's for. I think that's important. It breaks down barriers and builds trust. I'll drive two hours for lunch just to show someone that I care. It shows people that I respect them.

Meeting people where they are is trust-building at its core. Can you share an example of when that paid off significantly?

For the Amazon Web Services project that we announced a while ago, I worked on it for six or seven years with a good friend of mine who heads up site selection for them. I started going to Seattle and spending time with him and his team to learn more about the project. I've always done that. I will go see someone if they are willing to have me. That's one of the things that has helped my career more than anything else.

I'm with you. I love getting out and meeting people in their own communities, seeing their personalities shine and their points of pride. It's one of the gifts of working in this field. Including you, Ed. You know your business, and you're a lot of fun to hang out with.

It has been much more fun because I get to talk to people about what they like. That's just my approach. I seem to get along with people a lot better now that I talk about things they want to talk about, versus selling and pitching.

Do you have any advice for someone dealing with a local leader who is... Let's put this mildly... a troublemaker?

A good friend of mine in the site selection industry says that there is one of those people in every community where he goes. I'm thinking of a particular high-ranking leader in our realm from several years ago who was notoriously hard to work with. He didn't have a community development background, and he wanted to be the brightest star in the room. So, I did whatever it took to brief him first before anyone else. It made him feel valued and gave him the chance to be the most supportive person out there if he chose to be.

You've offered such good granular tactics, Ed. Thank you! Before we end, can you share any other advice?

Be ultra-responsive. That's what we try to do as a team: respond to people very quickly. It's funny because the people on my team now get frustrated when others don't operate that way. We may not have the information, but we'll tell you immediately that we will work on that.

Also, show up. Don't cancel last minute. If you said you were going to go, go. If you said you were going to do a call, do the call. We build trust when people know they can count on us.

27
JENNIFER WAKEFIELD

President and CEO, Greater Richmond Partnership

Richmond, Virginia

Trust Strengths

Reliability, Authenticity

"Trust is the foundation of relationships, and this is very much a relationship business."

Jennifer is the president and CEO of the Greater Richmond Partnership (GRP). In her role, she collaborates with public- and private-sector stakeholders to set and drive the organization's vision. She serves on the Richmond Federal Reserve Industry Roundtable, the University of Richmond Robins School Executive Advisory Council, the City of Richmond Economic Vitality Advisory Committee, the I-64 Innovation Corridor Research Council, and the Japan-Virginia Society, and is part of the VCU Advanced Pharmaceutical Manufacturing Cluster Development Program.

Before moving to Richmond, Jennifer served as vice president of Marketing and Communications for the Orlando Economic

Development Commission (EDC). There, she worked on numerous transformational projects in the region, including the Amway Center, Dr. Phillips Center for the Performing Arts, Citrus Bowl, Lake Nona Medical City, SunRail, and the merger of the Orlando EDC and the Central Florida Partnership.

Jennifer has a master's degree in communications and a bachelor's degree in public relations and advertising. She holds the Accreditation in Public Relations (APR) designation. Jennifer is also a board member of the International Economic Development Council (IEDC). She has won numerous local, regional, national, and international awards for her work.

Jen, I'm so glad you agreed to an interview. I loved working with you on your latest strategy and am grateful for this time to hear your thoughts on the topic of trust. This has been on my mind for years now. You've seen it in play throughout your career, too. Can you help me rate it on a scale of one to ten?

I don't know if it's a ten, but it's a strong eight and a half or nine. It's absolutely critical.

Trust is the foundation of relationships, and this is very much a relationship business. It's transactional, but it's relationship-based. Like when Lego came to our region through a long-time relationship I had with a site consultant. He knew me, and he called me.

People who try to distance themselves and aren't authentic in their personal and professional lives are doing themselves a disservice. That's where fakeness comes in.

Jen, you're very good at juggling a lot at once. I would think authenticity is one of your top Trust Strengths. Any others?

I got into this field because I felt like I could truly be myself.

Again, like Lego locating here. Lego has a set called "Everyone Is Awesome." Through that, I was able to talk about my experience as a parent of a gender-non-conforming child and a special-needs child. And that comes into play because, guess what? We are all human.

I've watched you in action and seen your honesty with other people. Not everyone is that transparent.

I would always prefer that someone tell me straight like it is and to my face, rather than behind my back. And if I hear something someone said behind my back, which inevitably I will, I will call them on it, maybe even in front of others, because that's who I am now.

Jen, you've mentioned the Lego story a few times. Can you tell me about that win, or maybe another pursuit when trust played an important role?

Working on Amazon's HQ2 site search. That project was a pivotal turning point for our organization in building trust with our public- and private-sector partners. We worked together to make a case for the Richmond region to be the destination of their headquarters. And it was a very public, national search, so competition came from everywhere in America.

Also, when I took over as president here in 2021, it was a turning point for our organization. We updated our articles and bylaws and created value statements. Everything we have done has been bottom-up. We created committees.

It's like the strategic plan that you led last year. It came up from each of our committees. Everyone provided input. They can see themselves in it.

You mentioned HQ2, and I also think of the big COVID-era grants like Build Back Better. Do communities need an urgent opportunity like those to boost trust among local leaders?

Crises can be big turning points for communities. We've seen that as we look at best practices in other markets. I was in Orlando when the Pulse nightclub shooting happened. The community truly came together in the wake of the tragedy.

Greater Richmond hasn't had a crisis, which is a blessing, but we have gone after big projects like HQ2 with everything we've got. That brought people together.

Jen, what are some things your local leaders do to build trust with each other?

We have monthly calls with each of our local government partners. And I started having one-on-one time with each of them as well. It's getting to know each other more as people. And, when meeting with them, I try not to talk about work the entire time. The conversations are more like, "How is your family doing? Or your house renovation?"

Are you going to their office or meeting for coffee? What's the format?

We meet for lunch, mainly, and close to their office. Meet them in a space that they like to go. Every couple of months.

You mentioned the strategic planning process that we recently finished. Do you think that helped strengthen trust?

Yeah. I think strategic plans have an opportunity to bring people closer together. Among our local partners, making sure that we're doing what it is that they want us to do is critical. But also keeping in mind that we are a public-private entity and that it has equal parts representation from the public sector and the private sector.

Jen, is there anything else you want to share before you go back to your busy day?

You may have noticed before that I have "APR" after my name. That means "accredited in public relations." The main reason I got that is that I worked at a place a while ago where I had created one of the first innovative things in government, which was really cool. One of the elected officials spoke critically about it on an audiotape. When a member of the media asked me for the said audiotape, I was told, "Oh, no, it didn't record," which wasn't true. I found the tape and provided it to the media.

And then I waited to be fired. But I was not fired. Instead, I lost trust in that executive, and I chose to leave the job shortly after. That helped me win my APR. I was willing to put my job on the line to do what was right.

28
NATHAN OHLE

President and CEO, International Economic Development Council

Washington, DC

Trust Strengths

Reliability, Active listening

"Trust is the single most important factor in moving a project forward, even if it's underappreciated."

Nathan Ohle is an internationally recognized expert in economic development and currently serves as president and CEO of the International Economic Development Council (IEDC), a nonprofit, nonpartisan membership organization serving economic developers with more than five thousand members worldwide. In 2017, he was selected as one of the 40 Under 40 Rising Stars in economic development internationally.

Nathan's economic development experience and leadership span decades at the local, state, and federal levels. Before joining IEDC, Nathan was the chief executive officer of the Rural Community Assistance Partnership (RCAP), a national network of nonprofit partners working to build capacity in rural and tribal communities across the country. Nathan served as the senior advisor at the U.S. Economic Development Administration (EDA), overseeing policy and external affairs, and at the Michigan Economic Development Corporation.

Nathan, first of all, thank you for taking the time to meet with me. I know there are just a few small things going on in DC right now, which is why I have been looking forward to this interview. You bring the national perspective, observations from the thousands of economic developers and community leaders who are members of IEDC, and practices from within your own organization.

So, let's dive in. On a scale of one to ten, how important is trust in economic and community development?

Can I say above ten? It seems like an obvious thing, but it might be one of the more undervalued aspects of our work. I have a vantage point among folks across a wide swath of America. I think trust is the single most important factor in moving a project forward, even if it's under-appreciated. For the future of our field, everything starts and ends with it.

Can you elaborate on that? Let's just say it's an 11 out of ten.

I think about economic developers who take a position in a new community at a new organization. If you're new to a community, you start by building trust. You can't come in with a ton of ideas immediately because, if you haven't built trust as a local, nothing's going to take off.

So, trust is important from the beginning. And then you have to maintain trust longer term and know how to repair it when it's broken to continue progress. When trust is broken, nothing will get done.

I like how you break it down into those three stages: building trust anew, maintaining it, repairing it. Can we talk about each one and specific things people can do in each? Let's start with advice for people who are in a new role in a new place.

It starts with showing up, being very transparent, and focusing on learning. Many people come in and say, "How can you help me?" Instead, say, "I want to learn why you are here and how I can help." That starts with coffee conversations, showing up to community events, and having one-on-one meetings.

Maybe most importantly, listen and find ways to act on what you hear. This can be small, like following through on something they mentioned or finding a way to support them publicly or privately. Doing that work in the first six months is critical.

I can tell that you're speaking from experience. You've been with IEDC for three and a half years now. When you arrived there, did you have a plan in place for your first six months? And what did it look like once you got there?

Yes, I had a plan. Based on my experience, I knew what was effective and what was not. My plan was to meet with every one of my team members in the first thirty days and every one of my fifty-five board members in the first ninety days.

I had eighty-one one-on-one meetings in those first three months. I had three or four questions for each of them and told them they could ask anything about me and my goals. It was very intentional. I asked them about how they are showing up, what they are doing, their ideas for what we could do better, and ways I could best support them. And I took a few of those ideas and started implementing them so they could see that I listened and wanted to help.

Then I did the same thing with external partners.

We didn't change much in the first three months, but we started forming relationships and building a framework. I showed them that we wanted to be true partners and that we were committed to them for the long run.

I had 425 meetings in my first year.

Incredible. A clear commitment to build trust from the start. How have you continued to foster that trust since then?

It's about creating a regular cadence for those meetings. For example, I meet with everyone on my team and board once a year, in person.

One of the other things that I do is help people understand how I operate. About six months in as CEO, I realized that my asking questions might be scary to the team. It wasn't part of the previous culture. So, I put together a Nathan-only user guide explaining the way I work and my expectations. For example, if I send you a report, I expect you to send it back redlined, and I will do the same for you. It's not because there is a problem; it's because that's the way I show up. I will be transparent and give feedback, and you should, too.

Another example: I meet with our partners every quarter, or twice a year, just to share ideas without an agenda. I want to hear their feedback on how we can improve.

Even after my first year, my average is 375 meetings a year.

Amy, it was the same thing when we worked with you and your team on IEDC's strategic plan. We wanted a lot of input.

Yes, I loved helping you and the team shape the strategy. We heard from almost nine hundred people.

It was important to me that everyone had a voice. And everything we do as an organization is based on a strategic plan.

That is music to my ears, Nathan!

Another specific thing, and it's a small thing, but I respond to emails. If I get an email from you, you will hear back from me, often within a couple of hours. Right now, I only have twelve emails in my inbox.

So, you're a member of the clean inbox club? I'm very impressed.

I want to talk to you about the third stage of trust building you mentioned earlier: fixing trust when it's broken, or even changing a culture that's different from yours. Any specific advice on that subject?

"Yes" to the question about changing culture. It started with meetings with the team. Letting them know that change was going to happen.

Being supportive and committed to helping them. If someone isn't a fit with the organization, I will help them find what their next thing is going to be.

It's funny. One of my team members asked me, "When does change stop?" I said, "The change never stops." Change is part of life, and it's part of growing an organization in a field that is constantly evolving. We must evolve, too. If people feel like they are a part of the change and their voices are heard, then they will help champion it.

What advice would you give to another leader who needs to bring their community along through rapid change?

Often, economic developers are caught in the world between people who understand what they do and those who don't. They find ways to bridge the gap between the two. Sometimes, they can do that alone, and sometimes, they should bring in a third party to help.

One of the most undervalued attributes of economic developers is their ability to tell a story. With such a vast array of constituents, the messages must be tailored to the audience. Those who know how to do that well connect with people and build trust in deeper ways.

One thing I'm asking interviewees is to think about their own trust-building skills. Of the eight Trust Strengths I shared, are there one or two that are totally Nathan?

I think active and adaptive listening is number one, with the added piece about following up and providing feedback on what I heard.

Then, I think number two is showing up, reliability. I show up a lot. It's really important to me. This isn't going to be a one-off conversation. I'll consistently show up.

I would love to give you a few minutes back in your day. To wrap up, I have a final question. Can you share an example in which trust led to significant progress in a community?

I can think of a lot of examples, but the one that comes to mind is what has happened in West Virginia. Historically, they struggled, but over the course of the past five years, they have started to talk to each other.

It began with a handful of local leaders facilitating conversations about how they can't keep doing things the same way. They didn't know where it would go at first, but then they started thinking regionally. Eventually, it led to significant growth and funding. For example, they've leveraged more than $100 million in funding over the last few years. The trust they fostered helped them successfully compete for those funds.

One of the other Trust Builders I've interviewed is Brandon Dennison with Coalfield Development Corporation.

Yes, he is one of those leaders. Also, Donna Gambrell, who runs Appalachian Community Capital. When she shows up and says that they won't provide capital unless people work together, that's a powerful incentive.

Nathan, thank you for your time today. Any last words of wisdom?

Building trust is about showing up, listening, following up, and being yourself. These are things that everyone can do, no matter your job.

But the thing is that it takes a lot of time. People might question the value of taking a lot of time to do this, but every minute is worth it. It helps you understand who you can work with and who you can't work with, and it sparks ideas that lead to better opportunities.

29

PETER CHAPMAN

President and CEO, One Neighborhood Builders

Providence, Rhode Island

Trust Strengths

Reliability, Respecting differences

"You can't begin to build real trust if you aren't addressing very real needs in a tangible way."

Peter is a visionary and multifaceted economic and community development executive and advisor. His achievements have been recognized by the American Planning Association (APA) and the International Economic Development Council (IEDC). He has over twenty years of progressive leadership and executive-level management experience with private, NGO, public, and non-profit institutions that conduct city and regional development through sector-based business attraction and expansion, global commerce, real estate revitalization, the planning and financing of housing, and assistance for underrepresented entrepreneurs and emerging real estate developers. He has served as a community development executive in places like Rhode Island, the U.S. Virgin Islands, Detroit, Norfolk, Richmond, and Denver. His consulting practice, Urban Policy Innovations, has been a go-to advisor for nearly twenty years.

Peter, we've worked together as strategists on multiple projects over the years. In addition to your consulting work, you've led community development work in places across the U.S. and Caribbean before your current role in Rhode Island. It's nice to sit down with you to hear about your take on trust building, considering your vast experience.

What role does trust among local leaders play in moving the needle, so to speak?

It's important. Along the way, I've learned that if you're working in a place where there is a history of dysfunction and disinvestment, you can't put forth vision and models that will overwhelm the people you're working with on the ground. You can't want transformative change more than local leaders want it.

I don't think that anyone who's worked with me would say I take community development lightly. I'm very serious. Maybe sometimes I'm too serious about bringing my all, trying to implement best practices. You can engender goodwill and try to build trust, but at the end of the day, it's whether local leaders want to make an impact.

I get it, Peter. And the opposite is true. Communities that have a history of success have more confidence and are willing to jump into bigger and bigger community projects.

Yes, you want to meet local leaders where they are. Give them opportunities that match where they are in their thinking. For example, sometimes, leaders in secondary and tertiary markets have been conditioned not to believe in their own capabilities and potential for growth and evolution.

Building trust might be more complex than doing a hardcore economic development strategic plan. Trust is built in the execution.

Do you think "trust" is an easier concept to believe in at the regional level than the hyper-local level?

If you're talking to groups that are involved in place-based community development, like the nuts and bolts of housing, they're dealing with in-the-trenches needs. I can tell you that stakeholders at that neighborhood level often don't have a lot of trust. They don't believe regional stakeholders are operating in their interests.

Peter, I want to hear about your personal experience building trust in place-based organizations and with their stakeholders. How exactly do you foster trust among people who are, like you said, in the trenches?

For example, my current organization is an affordable housing development organization. We noticed it's one thing to build housing. But if the neighborhood economy is weak and local businesses aren't healthy, no one benefits.

To address this, we created a microfinance fund. It's largely targeted to entrepreneurs of color to provide them with customized, patient capital and low interest rates. It meets their immediate need for capital, and it's given us a platform for more meaningful dialogue about more comprehensive economic development. It's still fairly new, but it has helped engender a lot of trust. It addresses their needs in real time.

The lesson here is you can't begin to build real trust if you aren't addressing very real needs in a tangible way.

How do your personal experiences contribute to trust building?

As an Afro-Latin American, I have cultural relationships. It helps with connecting and communicating. As I said earlier, you can't be way out in front of them with a vision or program that they just don't get and don't believe you relate to.

Was there a moment at the beginning of the microfinance program where you brought people together? What did that look like on the ground as you kicked off?

The first phase was a needs assessment. We brought small businesses together with other community leaders to have a conversation. In both English and Spanish, I'll add. That was important. We asked about their daily needs. Much of the input was around the need for capital. They didn't have the resources to buy inventory or make façade improvements, for example.

That was the beginning of the Central Providence Community Loan Fund. We created a structure and brought in a Community Development Financial Institution (CDFI) and a partner to help us administer the program.

Part of building trust was listening first and then executing on what we heard. Listening is very, very important. The folks in these neighborhoods are non-white and multilingual. There are the things I do during the workday, and then I have after-hours meetings with the people who are at work in the neighborhoods. Hearing their concerns about where they are builds trust.

I totally appreciate the need to listen, but it's impossible to listen to every single person in the community. How do you decide who to include?

I use intermediaries. For my first few months in a new community role, I'll spend time getting a sense of who has street cred. I try to connect with those individuals to validate intel that I've heard from other stakeholders. I work from there. But, yes, start with credible intermediaries.

In our strategy work, we take similar paths to make inroads with the mainstream business community. It can be a little messier when you're working with grassroots constituents, but the process is almost the same.

You have a broad range of experience, Peter. What do you do to build trust with a team that you haven't worked with before?

I spend my first few months doing good reconnaissance on who is out there, who has a platform to access, and building trust with key stakeholder groups. I might start with anchor institutions, like universities, hospitals, or the real estate community. People working at the top of the food chain.

Then, based on the community we are investing in—it could be geographic or ethnic—I try to identify the folks within that constituency who can help me forge relationships with others.

I try to appeal to different stakeholders based on my background. On my dad's side, roots go back literally to seventeenth-century England. That helps find a common thread in certain communities. When I go to other markets, I might share that my mom's family is 100 percent Panamanian and Barbadian. Other places don't have as intensive racial divisions and differences, and my background doesn't come into play as much.

Essentially, I can use my personal story in different ways to begin the process of building trust. But the strategy differs based on the dynamics of each community.

Some of my interviewees have brought up the difference between trust building in transactional communities versus relational communities. Any perspectives on that?

Certain communities have a different dominant culture in how they go about problem-solving. There might be significant differences in how they define and address problems.

For instance, in Denver, there is a culture of welcoming change. It might be related to their frontier mentality. Historically, survival hinged upon the ability to partner up with neighbors. A different culture emerged there than in other places that associate economic development with very specific industries. Think tourism, oil, automotive, and others.

There is a steeper learning curve in those industry-dominant places. Like, "Why do we need to change our model?" It can be more difficult to penetrate the community.

Do you think a generational change can help expand that mindset?

It's partly generational, but there is a cultural dimension to it. There might be conditioning where the same viewpoints from the older generation get recycled.

It reminds me of Michael Porter's book, *The Competitive Advantage of Nations*. It's a phenomenal piece of work. Why do some communities succeed while others fail?

Agreed, Peter. We're still discussing Dr. Porter's principles. His work has been that impactful.

I know there were concerns that it was culturally biased, but challenging communities to think about their competitive advantages and how they align with the global market is a wake-up call for some places, and it continues today.

Peter, I could talk with you for hours, and this has been an inspirational conversation. But I want to respect your time, and I have a final question for you. Circling back to my first question, to what degree does trust play a role in community prosperity?

It's the central question. I look at it through the lens of disinvested communities. Ultimately, their progress will be more sustainable if trust is built among local leaders. They have to lead the charge in economic development. And it's not just about business attraction. It's about creating an entrepreneurial class, physical redevelopment, and placemaking.

30

CATHY CHAMBERS

Economic Development Professional

Juno Beach, Florida

Trust Strengths

Respecting differences, Authenticity, Active listening

"I've seen that trust is not something you can develop overnight. But you can lose it overnight."

Cathy Chambers has worked for thirty years in utility and regional economic development in both Ohio and Florida. She has dedicated her career to recruiting companies that create jobs and invest capital in the communities she serves. Cathy has been named one of North America's Top 50 Economic Developers by Consultant Connect and honored as one of Florida Trend's 500 most influential business leaders in Florida. She holds a bachelor's degree in public administration from Miami University (OH) and a master's degree in business administration from Xavier University.

Hi, friend! As you know, I am interviewing local leaders across the country to hear their thoughts on trust. I'm testing the premise that

trust is the most important factor in economic development. That's where I'd like to start with you. On a scale of one to ten, how would you rank it?

It's on the high end of the scale, an eight, nine, or ten. I thought about it through the lens of fundraising, places that have been able to get a sales tax increase, infrastructure dollars, or even marketing resources. The places where those efforts succeed typically have high levels of trust among local leaders.

Think about the Better Jacksonville plan in 2000. The half-cent sales tax was designed to raise $2.5 billion for infrastructure and public facilities. I believe it passed because Mayor Delaney at the time was super-inclusive and built trust around the table. There was something in the package that helped everyone win. He was strategic.

I've seen that trust is not something you can develop overnight. But you can lose it overnight.

You're reminding me of a nerdy aspect of this book. I hope to correlate economic performance with indicators of trust. Those indicators are tricky to quantify. Any suggestions?

I think you'll find an above-average correlation with communities that have bigger budgets for economic development. Fundraising requires trust.

I want to hear about your strengths as a Trust Builder. Of the eight Trust Strengths that I shared, which ones are most Cathy?

It's funny, I thought of it almost on a continuum. I had a Midwestern upbringing in a Catholic family. When I started my career, being authentic and reliable were my strengths because those were Midwestern values.

I've also been big on the golden rule of treating people like I want to be treated. I try to meet people more than halfway because I think it gets things moving further, faster, building rapport and relationships. As my leadership journey progressed, I had to develop a real empathetic approach and respect differences. You know, stopping to honor people and actively listening to them. Those skills have developed over time.

You're the first Trust Builder I've interviewed who talked about this in terms of a continuum. When we're early in our careers, showing up, being ourselves, and doing good work is sometimes all we can do. But as we mature and our relationships grow, we can hone in on skills like active listening and empathy.

Right. Like, that can be a hard part when you're younger. It could even be difficult to be part of a conversation when you're meeting someone with a high-ranking position, for example. I am a fast talker and fast thinker. I had to train myself to take a beat, relax, and listen.

What are some specific things that you do to build trust with your team and other community leaders?

For the team, being in person is so important. We're back in the office five days a week, and I'm happy about it. I know not everyone loves it. But they understand that they can't feel the same passion and connectedness if they aren't in the same space with their team. I don't think you can ever really build trust if you don't spend time communing.

It's also about keeping things apolitical as much as possible because politics can be so divisive and immediately break down trust. I love that our work can be apolitical because both sides care about having a strong economy.

I think about a strategic planning process like the ones you lead, Amy. If you're effectively communicating what the process is and you're providing space for everyone to come together and truly contribute, you agree on what success looks like, and everyone has a role to play in implementing it. That helps build trust, and almost everyone can be happy.

Bingo! That's the secret. Inclusive planning and implementation.

Or the opposite. I've seen organizations start strategic plans with a lot of data and by bringing people together. They listen, but then nothing happens. Then people become disengaged and have zero trust in that organization going forward. Their doing nothing is misery.

Cathy, I'd like to hear your thoughts on celebrating wins. Assuming the culture of trust is healthy, and a major community project comes to fruition, or there is a significant new business expansion, how can you use that winning moment to reinforce trust?

A lot of effort goes into ribbon cuttings and photos, and those moments matter to a lot of people. So, first, it's really important to celebrate the wins.

You need to acknowledge people's contributions to those wins, but sometimes, the visible credit goes to people who weren't involved with the day-to-day. I never minded that as a professional. That's part of being an economic developer. Not being in the spotlight helps maintain the trust.

What advice would you share with younger people on their journey to becoming a community leader and Trust Builder?

A few things. Storytelling has been a big part of my leadership development. I think about all the presentations that are done, the data dumps. There's a better way.

You can build trust in a presentation environment. I try to find a story to tell during my presentations, especially one coming from a vulnerable place, like a personal story. I think about that a lot now in what I'm sharing and how I'm showing up. Making things more personal. Anyone can layer in their personality, even if they're there just to present data.

Another thing, and we mentioned it earlier, but a big thing that's missing is people doing what they say they will do. Just following up sets you apart. And that's a great way to build trust. It's just not as common as it used to be.

Why aren't people following through as much these days?

It's the phone generation, I guess. If it's not a text, it's just not going to happen. I still try to take time to write handwritten thank-you notes.

Do you think social media is impacting trust among community leaders?

Yes. Just look at the misinformation out there. Also, there is an attention span issue. Do people have the attention span needed to have a civil conversation on a complex matter? I miss those meaningful times with others.

I do, too. These Trust Builders interviews have been a delight. It's so rare to have time to dig in deeper with people and understand the ways they work. Much of my strategy work is gathering facts and opinions. I don't often get to sit down with leaders like you and learn about their character. Thank you for sharing your time and wisdom with me.

31

TANIA MENESSE

President and CEO, Cleveland Neighborhood Progress

Cleveland, Ohio

Trust Strengths

Respecting differences, Authenticity, Active listening

"By being willing to show your own weaknesses, your own vulnerabilities, the mistakes you've made, the challenges you faced... people will trust and open up to you. We will honestly say something isn't working with one of our neighborhood partners. We will say that not everything is perfect. But we will also advocate and defend them. Let's rally around and help them fill those gaps. That combination of honesty and support helps build trust."

Tania Menesse is the CEO and president of Cleveland Neighborhood Progress (CNP), an intermediary whose mission is to foster the equitable revitalization of neighborhoods throughout Cleveland by strengthening the community development ecosystem. The organization's first priority is to ensure that the city's community development corporations have access to the financial resources, talent, industry expertise, and technical assistance they need to effectively serve their neighborhoods.

CNP's work as an intermediary focuses on systems-level interventions, advocating for neighborhood change at all levels of government, raising capital, fostering real estate development, and telling the story of Cleveland's neighborhoods.

Menesse serves on the boards of Destination Cleveland, Ideastream, Digital C, Western Reserve Land Conservancy, and the Greater Ohio Policy Center and is a member of the Levin College Visiting Committee and the CDA Community Advisory Committee. She grew up in Shaker Heights and moved back to Cleveland twenty years ago with her family to focus her career on the revitalization of Greater Cleveland.

Tania, we first worked together in 2021 when we assisted with CNP's strategic plan. I know that you are a well-respected and highly trusted leader. To start, how do you describe the role trust building plays in the work that you do?

There's a great quote that says, "Leadership is literally showing up." I think what is moving Cleveland forward now is the fact that there are a lot of trusted relationships and people who are working with a lot of transparency and coming to the table.

But there are neighborhoods here where trust has been broken. People in those communities can't see themselves in progress or embrace it because, for literally decades, traditional institutions haven't come through for them. That means that progress can take a lot longer because we are starting from a different place.

To that, I just say, "We'll keep coming back. I know you don't feel good about this right now, and that's okay. I'm not going to try to convince you of anything. But I promise we will just continue to show up, and hopefully, at some point, our actions will speak much louder than words." For me, part of trust building is that: showing up and doing what I say I will do.

Can we drill down into that for a bit? How do you show up?

I try to show up authentically. My work is all about reputation and relationships. If people don't believe what I'm saying is what I truly believe, that I have integrity, then I really don't have anything. I don't have incredible technical talent, but I really care about people and have the patience to help move a community forward, even if it takes a long time. Again, I will keep showing up as my authentic self and wait for people to embrace change. It won't work if I impose it.

One example is that I admit that I don't have the same lived experience as some of the people we work with. I have been blessed to have food, shelter, and safety throughout my life. Others have not. So, I understand if they are leery about the programs we offer. They fundamentally don't believe that a home repair grant could be free because, during the foreclosure crisis, many of them lost their homes to predatory lenders. We have a lot of ground to make up, and that starts with me listening, being authentic, and being honest with them.

You've been in your position as president of CNP for five years, and before that, you were with the City of Cleveland. What tips can you offer about building trust with a new team, especially when you've been put in charge?

It can be hard being the new leader. Before CNP, I had not led my own organization. I came in admitting that I didn't know everything. I hadn't worked with a board of directors before, for example. But I committed to creating an incredible culture. I want to create a space where people feel valued, empowered, and heard.

I believe we have achieved that in a lot of ways over the past four years. A lot of it comes from helping our team members see each other's strengths and value each other's work, even if they might not see eye to eye on some things. A strong culture like this is more important than strategy. It means we can solve problems together, whatever comes our way.

Tania, I've seen you in action and admire your listening skills. Can you share some tips on how to be a great active listener?

I'm really glad you said that because I think it's an important part of trust building. I am genuinely curious and find people very interesting. I don't think you could fake that. I am learning that more and more every day, and I love it. Listening is critical to getting our work right.

I think you see people, and I'm guilty of it, too, who are kind of just waiting for someone to stop talking so they can make their next point. I try really hard to ask more questions and resist adding my two cents too quickly. I really want to make sure that others speak first so that I don't unduly influence what they're saying and so that I really hear them.

This helps in leading a team, too. Back to building a trustful culture, it creates an environment with people where they know that you actually want to hear them and that what they think is important.

Do you have any other words of wisdom related to trust building in work at the neighborhood level?

I think by being willing to show your own weaknesses, your own vulnerabilities, the mistakes you've made, the challenges you faced… people will trust and open up to you because they know you've walked a mile in their shoes. They know you have felt the panic and the pain and the struggle.

That honesty comes into how we relate to the organizations that we support. We will honestly say something isn't working with one of our neighborhood partners. We will say that not everything is perfect. But we will also advocate and defend them by pointing out that they may not have the tools or the dollars to perform better. So, let's rally around that to help them fill those gaps. That combination of honesty and support helps build trust.

32

HARVEY SCHMITT

CEO, Schmitt Consulting, and President Emeritus, Greater Raleigh Chamber of Commerce

Raleigh, North Carolina

Trust Strengths

Respecting differences, Integrity

"Getting through the political junk that we deal with today makes this work even more important. It's harder to do, but if you can find the people who have responsibilities and get them in an environment where they feel comfortable, you have a chance."

Harvey was president and CEO of the Greater Raleigh Chamber of Commerce from 1994 until 2015, when he became president emeritus. Prior to that, he served as president and CEO of the Greater Tampa Chamber of Commerce, president and CEO of the Greenville, South Carolina, Chamber, and in other positions. He is regarded as one of the most transformative chamber of commerce leaders of the past four-plus decades. He continues to serve communities through his firm, Schmitt Consulting, and as a member of the board of advisors of TowneBank.

Harvey, thank you for making time for this interview. I've been told by another interviewee that you are the most important person to hear from in this process.

To begin, I'm testing my premise that trust among local leaders is the single most important factor in economic and community development. Does that theory have legs?

I think it's spot on.

A lot of times, we create some sort of organizational infrastructure or hierarchy to force working together. I think informal is better for building trust. The more formal you get, the more people get in the weeds. The more informal you are, the more you can stay on the top-line items. If you get too pedantic about what the structure looks like, then the bean counters get into the conversation. You don't want that.

What are some characteristics of a productive informal approach to solving community issues?

You need a regular cadence of communication. For example, there are twelve chambers of commerce in Wake County. We would meet with those chambers once every quarter. You can fake sincerity, but you can't fake being there. I needed to show up to indicate that this is important.

Likewise, the four big chambers in the region would also meet once a quarter. I made sure I was there. And the economic development group, too. We would go to the Research Triangle Partnership once a month and meet with the Foundation, Durham, Chapel Hill, and us.

Those meetings weren't overly structured. There were opportunities to build social capital among the players.

Then, at the community level, on the first Friday of every month, we hosted the mayor, city manager, county commission chair, county manager, superintendent, CVB, downtown alliance, airport, and others. We had a three-minute egg timer, and each person gave an update. The most important part of it took place in our parking lot afterward, where they would continue to talk. We created a safe haven where people with differences could connect.

How much of your time as chamber president was dedicated to those meetings with local leaders?

It was significant, 20 to 25 percent of my time. But I always felt that I didn't have any inherent power myself. My power was being able to know what was happening in a lot of different places and being a trusted partner.

If you want to have trust, you must start by being trustworthy. That means you have to be consistent.

Consistency, yes. What are some other characteristics of trustworthy leaders?

Openly communicating is important, too. And being there. Not sending a proxy. If you send a proxy, then you're sending a message that it's important but not that important.

And don't be half-assed. When you are, then you are going to create cracks. And once there is one crack, it's easy for people to go back to bad behavior.

I'd like to hear more of your thoughts on communicating. I'm sure that's a big part of leading a chamber of commerce.

I always believed that in the absence of information, people assume the worst. To overcome that, you have to create a network of constant communication.

It's human nature to assume the worst. And that goes both ways. I used to tell my staff, "It's entirely possible that we don't know what's going on." So, we shouldn't assume. And we need to be straight up about the communication process. Don't get into a process of assuming bad intentions by people when it could simply be that someone isn't connected.

I agree. That can cause serious breakdowns. In your career, you've worked in three very successful regions. How did you effectively

communicate with and connect so many local leaders within those regions?

Yes, I led chambers of commerce in Tampa-St. Pete-Clearwater, Greenville-Spartanburg-Anderson, and then Raleigh-Durham-Chapel Hill. There were multiple economic development agencies and political bodies in each community. Trying to get everyone working together in a regional context required a lot of effort.

I was always in the largest market in those regions, so I felt that communication was my responsibility. I thought, *You need to communicate proactively and take responsibility for that. If it doesn't happen, it's your problem, not theirs.*

It takes a lot of tension out of the conversation because people aren't acting because they don't have enough information. You can sift out what's a bad actor and what's just bad communication.

It makes sense that the larger chamber in the largest market would take the lead in communicating and convening, especially if there is no regional entity.

If you're leading the chamber in a larger market, there might be partners in smaller markets who feel intimidated by the relationship. It's the responsibility of the larger market to create a comfort zone.

When I came to Raleigh, the Raleigh-Durham dialogue was terrible. Raleigh would articulate assets in its marketing materials that were really Durham's without properly putting them into a context or telegraphing what they were going to do. So, we came up with an internal marketing conversation called "family of communities" that involved the local chambers and the convention and visitor bureaus within the region. We agreed that some issues were not family issues and some were. Concentrate on family issues, like economic development, and each family member has their own personality characteristics.

It took eighteen to twenty-four months to get to a place where everyone would agree to make the distinction between having a family and not every family member having the same personality. We're not all alike, and that's okay.

How did you initiate those conversations, Harvey? You were new on the scene, there was dysfunction, and you realized a need to be more cohesive. What were your first steps?

I'd been through similar dynamics in my prior two regions. I think part of the reason I got the job in the first place was because I had experience in that space. Leadership understood that there was a constant conflict in the community. Wasted energy. Trying to figure out where the furniture was supposed to be placed as opposed to looking at the big picture.

I started the conversation about how we could create a regional transportation organization. That got all the mayors involved in economic development. But again, the communication process between those entities hadn't been strong in the past. I put structure on that. Almost all of what I was doing was about creating a consistent communication regimen. My organization served as the convener, but we didn't monopolize the conversation, nor did we try to leverage the conversation in a way that served our own agenda.

I would cover expenses so that people could focus on the real conversation, not arguing about who was paying their fair share. In the case of the regional work around brand identity, we paid for the agency. With the regional transportation organization, we covered the whole cost of studies and planning. We didn't ask the others for support, but everyone could sit at the table as an equal.

My final question for you, Havey: How has trust building changed over the years?

That's a good question. You know, I've been out of the business for eight years. But I think if you talk to my successor, she'll say that some of the communication structures I put in place are still in play. The leaders continue to meet on the first Friday of every month, for example.

Getting through the political junk that we deal with today makes this even more important. It's harder to do. But I still think that breaking bread together is a good thing. So are inner-city visits. An enormous amount of social capital is created when you have 120 leaders together for two to three days. They're flying out together, riding the bus together, eating together. Good things come out of that.

It's harder to do today because people aren't talking with each other. I don't know how you get over negative social media or talk radio. I don't know how you get past a lot of things out there. But if you can find the people who have responsibilities and get them in an environment where they feel comfortable, you have a chance.

33
STEPHEN CAUSBY

Associate Director, Grantmaking and Implementation, Park Pride

Atlanta, Georgia

Trust Strengths

Transparency, Integrity

"Trust your gut. If you are uneasy about having a certain conversation, ask yourself why. It is likely that others feel the same way. Pretending everything is fine and moving forward might produce a result that isn't worth the time spent. Stop to assess and do the exploration work. Engage a diversity of perspectives in those uneasy conversations."

Stephen Causby is a city planner with eighteen years of experience working to build stronger, more equitable communities in Atlanta, Georgia. Having worked at the regional and local levels, Stephen has had the privilege of engaging with leaders at all levels to identify and address challenges that face cities. He led regional programs in Atlanta to engage top leaders in critical public policy issues and championed neighborhood efforts to expand parks and affordable housing. Stephen received a BA from North Carolina State University and a master's in city and regional planning from Georgia Institute of Technology. He is employed with Park Pride, a park advocacy organization in Atlanta.

Stephen, I've admired you since our work together on the Atlanta region's cATLyst strategy, especially your focus at the neighborhood level and your natural ability to include people from all different walks of life. I am excited about hearing your thoughts on trust building.

Thank you for that. During that strategy process, I realized that we needed to push to make something different than before. We leaders were aligned and supportive, and luckily, we had you and your team engaged.

That strategy was part of the inspiration for this book. There was a point in the planning process when you called me and asked me to come out to lead an open house in a county that was frequently left out of work like ours. Their input became a pivotal moment and shaped the strategy's top priorities.

It was a game-changer.

Stephen, you've worn a number of hats, including director of the Office of Housing and Community Development at the City of Atlanta. There's a trust component to so much of what you're doing. On a scale of one to ten, with ten meaning trust is the most important factor in community development, where do you rate it?

It's a ten. It's one of the most important factors that we deal with, especially in low- to moderate-income communities.

There can be a lot of mistrust in high-growth metros where you see housing values rising and community change happening at a quickening pace. It's harder if there aren't robust mechanisms for public input on how that change happens.

I'm asking each interviewee to reflect on their strengths as Trust Builders. Which of the eight Trust Strengths reflect your approach?

Being transparent is one of them. I have such a low tolerance for dishonesty. The more tap dancing, the more you lose trust.

For example, I think of the neighborhood revitalization work we're doing. I've lived in one of those neighborhoods for twenty years. When we hold conversations, we begin by acknowledging that we know there has been a history of broken trust. But we're back and listening.

What incremental steps have you taken to rebuild trust?

The work is ongoing. I start by inviting people into conversations. For one initiative, a big investment going into a neighborhood, I worked for six to eight months on the phone, visiting with neighborhood residents, asking them to show up and share their input on the initiative. I knew that there were a few local leaders who needed to be present; otherwise, it wouldn't be legitimate, so I also reached out to them.

In the middle of the process, a significant infrastructure break happened blocks away from them, which made rebuilding trust more difficult. They started feeling even more like their neighborhood was held together with Scotch tape and chewing gum. So, we brought in the point person for the infrastructure issue, trying to connect residents directly with city hall and helping them be more informed.

You mentioned the work is ongoing. Can you share some of the practical tactics you use to keep the residents engaged?

I have found that you need people who wake up every day thinking about the economies in local neighborhoods. Find the right person for the job. We have a terrific project manager who works daily on the process. She is very sensitive to the needs of the community and has done a lot of trust-building herself. Her emotional intelligence is very, very high, and she is committed to racial equity.

For the past year, we met with residents monthly and had an agenda to talk through. We leave a lot of time and space for residents to share their concerns and be honest with us about how this work is landing in their community. If we need to change our communications approach, for example, we listen to their advice.

We are now out of the planning stage, and the focus is on implementing plans that have already been adopted. We pulled all the projects from the adopted plans and shared the list. We ask the neighborhood's leaders for their input on priorities and phasing. We talk a lot about available resources, too. What's actually feasible?

Overall, communication is important. Admit to past stumbles. Have a cadence of regular correspondence with them. Like, if a blighted building is going to be demolished, they don't want to just look up and see a bulldozer at the end of their street. Let them know in advance.

I want to zoom in on something you said. These community meetings have clear agendas to discuss projects that are currently underway. Does that level of structure result in more participation by neighborhood residents?

Yes, it helps. And we have to be honest with them as well. The plans were completed several years ago. We can't just take a snapshot of the moment that the plan was written and then just do it over the next fifty years. We've got to reassess and reanalyze constantly. That means project scopes can change based on what we're hearing from residents.

Some of these residents have been at the table for years. They want to see real projects, know where the money is, and know how things will get done. The funding can be a point of contention because it's uncertain if dollars will continue to be available three-plus years from now. We are honest about that.

The likelihood of continued funding goes up when city leaders hear from them. What specific things do you do to help neighborhood leaders advocate for themselves?

Our project managers take on some of that. For example, when blighted properties come up in municipal court for review, the project manager I mentioned earlier will email an alert to neighbors. Then they will come to court and speak personally about the importance of eliminating dilapidated structures. She, herself, will show up, too, to remind officials that it ties into the mayor's revitalization vision.

Again, you need someone on your team who is on the ground, building relationships. Someone who will go to neighborhood meetings and remind people of programs or events that can support small businesses or revitalization projects. Help demystify the process, players, and funding streams.

One of my last questions for you, Stephen, is what advice would you share with others who want to build a trustful culture?

My advice is to trust your gut. If you are uneasy about having a certain conversation, ask yourself why. It is likely that others feel the same way. Pretending everything is fine and moving forward might produce a result that isn't worth the time spent. Stop to assess; do the exploration work. Engage a diversity of perspectives in those uneasy conversations.

I completely agree, Stephen. Before we go, do you have any parting words of wisdom?

People need to hear these stories, Amy, and need to be challenged by this. Trust is so vital, especially now. Just the pace of change and how we all build something together that is for everybody makes your Trust Builders work very important.

Thank you, Stephen. I really hope the stories I've collected for this book will lead to greater trust in our local communities. Stronger trust equates to stronger communities from the neighborhood level up.

34

DEBRA TEUFEL

President and CEO, Hutchinson/Reno County Chamber of Commerce

Hutchinson, Kansas

Trust Strengths

Transparency, Reliability

"Sometimes, I joke that most challenges can be solved by picking sweet corn. That's the most rewarding part of this work. We get to meet so many people, and it's not just about the transaction. The biggest gift of all is the people that we encounter along the way."

Debra Teufel has been the president/CEO of the Hutchinson/Reno County Chamber of Commerce since 2017, where she leads economic development and tourism and is on the board of directors of Growth Inc., which is developing a five-hundred-acre rail-served industrial site. Prior to assuming this role, she served as the director of public-private partnerships at the University of Oklahoma, vice president of the Greater Wichita Partnership, and director of Cowley First and the Sumner County EDC.

She is a Kansas native, holds a BA in business administration from Southwestern College, earned her CEcD in 2008 from IEDC, and is a graduate of the University of Oklahoma's Economic Development Institute. Debra is a founding member of Kids Collective, on the YMCA board, past chair of the Chamber of Commerce Executives of Kansas, chair-elect of the Kansas Economic Development Alliance, and on the board of the Heartland Economic Development Course of the University of Northern Iowa, where she has taught Managing EDOs and Ethics.

She lives in Hutchinson, Kansas, with her husband, David. They have four grown children and four grandchildren.

Debra, first of all, I've really enjoyed seeing you as a Trust Builder in action when I helped with the Elevate Reno County strategy earlier this year. I know you wear a lot of hats, and I can't wait to hear your thoughts on this subject. In your opinion, how critical is trust in economic and community development?

It's almost a ten out of ten. It's way up there on the spectrum of importance. You can take a community that seems perfect on the surface, but if you don't have leaders working together, you can get stuck.

Openness and acknowledging what is broken in a community takes trust and vulnerability.

That brings to mind a question that only a few interviewees have answered. I would love to jump into it with you. Can you tell me about a shortcoming you shared in a way that helped build trust with others?

It's not the easiest thing for people to do. But when you do it and create that culture where you're able to be open and honest with each other, it is a great way to build trust.

For example, one of our community's biggest challenges today is wages. Low wages hold back a great deal of discretionary spending, which leads to other cracks in the system. I found early on that using data to inform the wage conversation helps depersonalize it. That way, I can stand in front of other community leaders, including some of the lower-wage employers, and say that we have a problem and they are part of the solution. Having those tough conversations backed by numbers helps us address challenges.

I've gotten to know you over the past few months of the strategic planning process. It has been fun seeing your authenticity and honesty in full force. Of the eight Trust Strengths that I shared, which ones resonate with you?

To me, being authentic and being transparent are equal. Opening up about how you came to be. It isn't like we just landed in the CEO role in our organizations. We came up through the ranks, and that shaped us. So, being able to sit down with peers in the community and talk about those realities helps build trust.

Reliability is also high on my list of importance. I try to be a consistent voice at the table, reliably being there for tough conversations and talking with others in the community about solving challenges.

It's amazing how it's difficult for some people to be reliable. We've all been in situations where someone who's extraordinarily talented only participates part of the time. It doesn't matter how brilliant they are; people start to lose trust in them because they aren't consistent.

It's also helpful to have people in your circle of trust who see your flaws even when you can't and are willing to point them out. I'm thinking of one local leader in particular. We would meet regularly with each other. There was a meeting where he was planning an event, and I told him I wouldn't be able to be there, but I would send someone from my team instead. And he said, "That's that thing you do."

I was like, "What is that thing I do?" and he said, "You delegate." My initial reaction was that I know my own limitations. I try to consistently show up everywhere I can, but I get pulled in a lot of directions.

Yes, you lead both the chamber and the economic development initiative. I can imagine you have conflicting meetings every day, right?

Yes. Sometimes, an important meeting circumvents everything else. It's helpful to have someone in your corner, like a trusted colleague, that you can bounce things off of and who is also willing to see your weaknesses and speak the truth to you.

You know, Debra, delegating wisely is a positive trait. Not everyone is able to do that effectively.

Some people want to hold everything so close that they can't possibly do it all. And they might not have developed leaders within their team who confidently represent them.

That leads to another important aspect of trust building: instilling trust within your team so that they can take on challenges and speak on the organization's behalf.

That's a good point. How have you developed people on your team who can reinforce trust between the chamber and other community leaders when you aren't there?

It's important to mentor them. I think back to when I was early in my career. There were people who saw things in me that I didn't even see. They encouraged me to reach for the next rung on the ladder.

I want to build that confidence in my team. I want to give them opportunities to be out there, learning. I think it's important that we are continuous learners. People learn by doing, even when they're afraid. At first, when they join the team, they might be nervous about going to a meeting and saying, "I'm Debra for today." But the more we encourage them to be themselves and be reliable, the stronger they become.

It's great that we started talking about your team first. That's so you! But let's spend a few minutes on your personal approach.

You do it naturally when you're new to a community. You're meeting with various leaders, getting to know people, and establishing trusting relationships.

The harder thing is maintaining trust. Just when you think, *Oh, wow, this person and I have a great relationship, and we're going to work on this cause together*, the next thing you know, they're leaving. It's a challenge in this profession, actually. Turnover in these community roles is pretty high.

How does high turnover within community leadership positions affect trust?

It's an undercurrent that can hold back progress. People who have been in a community for a while might be leery of planting because they worry that the person might not be there long enough to carry out their ideas. It takes an incredible amount of cultural trust building to get past that within your team, board members, volunteers, public and private sectors, schools, and so many other partners. In the last eight years in our community, for example, we've had six city managers, four hospital CEOs, three school superintendents, two county managers, and two community college presidents.

It sounds like the lyrics to the song "The Twelve Days of Christmas." But joking aside, that puts a fine point on the fact that trust building is essential and ongoing. How have you done it?

At one point, we had a CEO group with executives from major employers, schools, the college, and high-ranking public officials. We met on a monthly basis to work on common goals and a shared vision. As it progressed, we realized it would behoove us to have an outside consultant to guide the conversations and document our vision. Having the frequency of that get-together held us accountable and reminded us of what we needed to work on. It became common nature to talk in terms of our shared community vision issues. We were on the cusp of rolling out some big initiatives, but then COVID happened.

So many great initiatives everywhere had to hit the COVID pause button. But here we are today, and you have a new strategic plan in the works.

Yes, and it's all starting up again. Childcare and housing are big areas of focus, along with making sure we have the sites and infrastructure to support growth.

Let's talk about the community's success in increasing childcare options countywide. I've been impressed with what you all have accomplished.

Childcare came up in most of our business conversations and surveys as a concern. But unless you dive into the data, it's hard to pinpoint what the problem is. Childcare groups had been meeting for a decade or more, but mostly they were childcare or education professionals. It wasn't a very holistic approach.

One day, I received a call from a business that said that they were affiliated with a nonprofit foundation. The founders wanted to make a big community gift but needed help focusing it. So, we formed a childcare task force and hired a professional to help quantify the problem for the donor. And right around that time, COVID relief dollars became available through ARPA. We were already organized and armed with data, and the nonprofit was at the ready. We went in together with a consistent fact-driven message. In turn, we were able to allocate a good portion of our ARPA funds to form our childcare nonprofit, Kids Collective, and expand capacity.

I've heard you use the term "speaking it into existence." That's when you have the microphone, you are open with audiences about the community's challenges, and people respond. It goes back to your strength as a Trust Builder: being transparent.

It works, too. I had been frequently speaking about the need to develop larger business sites when a chamber member called. He asked if I had a gift pledged to economic development to solve a community challenge, what would it be? They asked me to give them a menu of things to choose from and said that they had a million dollars in funding. If we had not built trust over the course of time, this offer might not have ever happened.

We had done some work to identify potential industrial sites but had not had a conversation with landowners to see how much a million dollars would stretch. While we worked on that, he was planting the seed with his neighbor, who was the potential gifter. Several months later, I got to meet the neighbor in person. I showed her the maps we had been working on and talked about the vision that her gift would lead to great things for our community.

It's giving me goosebumps to share this story. Without the trust of that chamber member, I would never have had the chance to get to know and appreciate Sharon Kimball. She had an economic developer's heart, and she wanted to do good things for the community that she loved. Our relationship with her led to more trust building with neighbors who have since sold or optioned land to us.

All the puzzle pieces seemed to have fit together, Debra. It sounds like trustful personal connections are at the center of it all.

That's right. And it led to a relationship with the owner of the neighboring piece of ground. I lined up the details for optioning his family's property and hosted a meeting with them, our board chair, and the support team. They were longtime members of the community. After one of our meetings with them, the family patriarch said that they would be picking corn the next day. He asked me if I would be interested in helping. I spent the next afternoon picking and shucking sweet corn with him and his family.

It took a lot of time and gathering other support to negotiate the option agreement on their property. But it wouldn't have happened without just sitting down and understanding what motivates people and knowing where they are coming from. Rolling up sleeves and working side by side with the family in the cornfield.

It goes back to those principles we talked about earlier around being oneself. I could see myself in this family. They are entrepreneurial, and they are a farm family. They attend a small church on the edge of town. I grew up on a family farm and attended a church on the edge of town. I think that they could see that I had the very same upbringing that they did. I felt like I understood what was important to them. It's probably the best lesson in life: be yourself. I believe most people are good, but sometimes, it takes just being oneself and opening up to be able to trust.

Sometimes, I joke that most challenges can be solved by picking sweet corn. That's the most rewarding part of this work. We get to meet so many people, and it's not just about the transaction. The biggest gift of all is the people that we encounter along the way.

Amen to that, Debra. And thank you. I'll never forget your story.

35

LORIE VINCENT

President, Acceleration by Design, and Founder, Stand Up Rural America Summit

Austin, Texas

Trust Strengths

Transparency, Reliability

"I communicate and engage people in times of calm. It's not a good time to start building partnerships and coalitions when things heat up for a big opportunity or crisis, and people panic. When an opportunity comes up, you want everyone to already know each other. It helps you get to work much faster."

Lorie Vincent is a certified economic developer with more than three decades of hands-on experience. Throughout her career, she has crafted high-impact organizational strategies, dynamic prospect events, and memorable marketing initiatives that have contributed to thousands of jobs and billions in capital investment. Having partnered with more than 450 cities involving twenty industries across the U.S. and abroad, she brings deep insight into economic trends and emerging opportunities.

Equally at home in cowboy boots and a hard hat or a suit and stilettos, Lorie has supported communities ranging from the smallest cities to the largest states. A sought-after speaker, strategist, writer, and trainer, she is known for her energy, expertise, and practical approach. A strong advocate for regionalism and rural America, she has a proven record of results.

Lorie is the author of the best-selling book *Stand Up Rural America*, with her second book, *Misadventures, Mishaps & Mayhem*, launching in the spring of 2026.

Lorie! Thanks for being a part of my project. This is a topic that's been on my mind for a long time.

I'm excited about this. I haven't seen anybody have this discussion before.

I hope it's helpful. I think it's an important topic nowadays.

To begin, I want to hear your thoughts on the correlation between trust among local leaders and community development.

I experienced that dynamic even in my first economic development job. They had recently established a county economic development group. When I interviewed for the job, the board admitted that they were new at this and we could learn together. They tasked me with finding ten aspirational cities and reporting back on what they are doing right and wrong. They were fantastic. The board was filled with doers in the community.

Since then, and I've been in this profession for thirty-five years, I've added ten cities to that list every year. My study now has over three hundred cities, with best practices in each. You can see trust at play in the ones that are most successful.

Can you rate trust on a scale of one to ten in terms of importance to community and economic development?

It's a nine or ten. A community has to have a common desire for progress and economic prosperity. But then trust needs to be strong because nothing will happen without it.

I've been in communities where there was trust but no desire to progress. They've never had a situation where trust has been broken. They haven't lost a project, they're rocking along, nobody is pushing a personal agenda, and there hasn't been controversy or corruption. So, trust is there; they just aren't pursuing economic development because they don't have that common desire. That apathy isn't because they don't care but because they don't share an interest in growth.

Lorie, before we get into examples of trust in action, I want to learn more about your strengths. You led a 69-county region in the Texas Panhandle, South Plains, and Permian Basin for seventeen years. That's a lot of miles. What about your personality kept trust among local leaders strong for so long?

I thought long and hard about this because all eight Trust Strengths that you sent are important to anyone in community and economic development. But for me, when you're serving a big region like mine, I learned to consistently communicate. People might even think that I overcommunicate. But I'll take that every day and twice on Sunday over someone saying, "I had no idea what Lorie was thinking." I don't want people wondering what I'm doing. I prefer to be transparent.

It's also about reliability. Showing up. I'm known as someone who will do what I say I'll do. That also means that I'm very careful about what I say I will do.

Your experience is so strong, particularly across Texas and now through your consulting work and Stand Up Rural America summits. What advice do you give local leaders who want to build trust?

I always give options. I acknowledge up front that there's more than one way to get from A to B. Instead of coming in and giving one option, acting like I'm the smartest person in the room, it has become very systematic for me to come up with a couple of options, and each option requires different resources, timing, and partners.

If you go into a community gathering or a city council meeting, no two people are going to think alike. So, if you give them options, there's a starting point for a discussion. And one option will eventually rise to the top.

Lorie, what are some specific things that you do to build trust? I want to hear the details.

I communicate and engage people in times of calm. It's not a good time to start building partnerships and coalitions when things heat up for a big opportunity or crisis, and people panic. When an opportunity comes up, you want everyone to already know each other. It helps you get to work much faster.

Think about the COVID pandemic. The communities that had strong relationships with their existing businesses and good trust among local leaders were able to react much more quickly and effectively. They also had more success competing for federal funding.

In practice, that means implementing a strong, local business retention and expansion program. I've often told my client communities, "Order a hundred breakfast tacos and deliver them to local businesses every day for a week. Thank them for being in business. Tell them, 'We see you, and we appreciate you.'"

Breakfast tacos can work magic, Lorie! Coming from Austin, I love it and totally agree.

I think I know the answer, but is there a risk of apathy setting in if you aren't engaging folks in times of calm?

Yes, especially if things are going well. Arrogance is fat and sassy and can become prevalent. That's why you need to continue building relationships when times are good. Those are the times when we build infrastructure and invest in community improvements. Calm times are when our plans and visions become so important.

You're so well-connected. Is there another community leader you admire who has a gift for trust building? And what do they do well?

Yes, it's Amanda Nobles. She's an expert at working with community leaders. And she's a great mentor. Amanda is a calming person. The town where she worked for thirty years prior to retiring has a tremendous amount of trust in her. That's because she always listened to every person who had a comment. She would say, "That's a great observation, and I will follow up." She would respond back to them within forty-eight hours.

Again, do what you say you're going to do, and people will begin to trust you. Show people that you heard them and reinforce positivity in your response.

In her career, they had some great wins and some challenges, like every place has. But she never let that get her down; she would just continue to work in her calm and consistent way.

Lorie, besides trust, are there any other secrets to a thriving community?

Always follow up. As a leader representing a large region, my team and I would go to industry events and bring home a list of companies interested in our region. I would send it to our local communities. But sometimes, the companies would let me know that the local communities never followed up with them.

It would be devastating to me. But then I started thinking, maybe some of these small towns just don't know how to follow up. So, we started an education program on how to respond to prospects. That means, even if the company didn't choose your town, send them a follow-up note thanking them for their time and attention.

Follow through on what you say you'll do. It seems like such a simple way to build trust. What a great reminder. Thank you, Lorie!

36

MAUREEN DONOHUE KRAUSS

President and CEO, Detroit Regional Partnership

Detroit, Michigan

Trust Strengths

Transparency, Reliability

"Spend a lot of time listening. One thing I learned along the way is that economic development has a different definition, no matter where you are. I'll ask, 'What is important to move this community ahead? What do people want? What don't they want?'"

Maureen spent over thirty years with her boots on the ground, starting as an intern in the industry and building her way up to an experienced economic development leader. From Michigan to Arizona to Indiana and back to Michigan, she has helped communities learn from the past, embrace the present, and find the path forward to a bright future. The Detroit region is especially near and dear to her heart. Maureen grew up in Southeast Michigan and has seen the community grow into the global leader it is today.

Prior to taking the helm at the Detroit Regional Partnership, she served as the CEO of the Indy Chamber and Indy Partnership, vice president of economic development at the Detroit Regional Chamber, and director of economic development at Oakland County, Michigan. Her bachelor's degree is from Albion College, and her Master of Public Policy is from the University of Michigan.

Maureen, to start off, I'm asking all of the interviewees to reflect on the role of trust in successful economies. On a scale of one to ten, how do you rate it?

It's a ten. I talk about this a lot when I'm speaking publicly or to my board. I was born here, and there are still people left in economic development who remember me when I was a college intern. I go way back with several of the communities in the region. I believe the reason that Detroit Regional Partnership and I have been successful in the past five years is because people know me and they trust me.

Having that trust with our public partners is essential, especially since, in the past, there was a lot of competition within the region. I've always said that all the communities in the region need to trust that Detroit is our calling card. If we combine our assets, we can win more. And we need to trust each other.

I'm thinking about a project from a couple of years ago. A large employer was consolidating, which meant one community in our region would gain jobs and another would lose jobs. The company asked us to manage the conversations. We were able to build trust in the process because we were upfront with the community about losing jobs. We talked to them about the move before it made headline news. No surprises. And we were able to help them fill the space that went vacant.

Can you share some specifics on how you build trust?

It's a funny thing because you have to be transparent but also keep things confidential.

How do you strike a balance between transparency and confidentiality? For example, another interviewee said that they don't sign

nondisclosure agreements because trust is so high among local partners.

We've had thoughts around that as well. We don't have a problem signing NDAs. We're obviously not a public sector organization, and our elected officials see our projects once they are pretty far down the road. Like when a company wants to locate in the region, we are speaking with them early on about sites. We're talking with local utility companies and workforce people. Later on, when we involve elected officials, they might be upset when we ask them to sign an NDA. They might worry that we're keeping stuff from them. But the reality is, we have to keep things confidential for the first phases of a project, or we risk the company locating somewhere else.

It's a balancing act, to your point. Detroit Regional Partnership covers a large territory and a wide diversity of communities. How do you keep everyone engaged?

We're an 11-county region with 348 cities, villages, and townships. We meet with each county every six months. We share what we're doing, what our calendar looks like, and our results. And most importantly, we listen to them: what their challenges are and the progress they are making.

We also assign a business development representative to each county. Each team member has two or three counties that they support. They'll attend the county's quarterly and annual meetings. Attend major community events. That sort of thing.

Can you share an example of how you keep your public sector partners energized about your work? They might be motivated differently than your private-sector partners.

We get them on stage whenever it's appropriate. For example, we are hosting a group of site consultants here in a few weeks. We scheduled breakfast for them with our top elected officials. It gives them a chance to talk about their unique communities and hear what the consultants have to say. Maybe they'll gain insights that will help them be more responsive or help with decisions.

I continue to communicate the message that we're all in this together. We need to compete as a region and not against each other locally. As you know, economies are regional. Talent is regional. Supply chain is regional. That's why we work regionally. We're competing for businesses and talent against other regions, like Atlanta, Columbus, and Indianapolis.

Competition is in our DNA. We have the Big Three automotive companies here, and they've always competed. But there has been a generational shift in leadership, and the new leaders differ from past ones, who may have thought we were all battling each other. Younger leaders are more willing to work together, set aside differences, and trust each other.

Detroit has a lot of buzz nowadays. It must be a fun time to be there!

The city has turned around, and everyone's proud of it. I live twenty-five miles north of the city, and I'm excited to come into work every day and see cranes in the air and so many things happening. Like today, I need to head home early because we have three sold-out Detroit Tigers games in a row this weekend, two theater productions, and other things going on. The place is jammed with people. It wasn't that way before, but now there is a great sense that this is a cool place. We survived. We survived bankruptcy. We survived the auto industry going bankrupt. We believed in ourselves, and now others have come along to be a part of it.

Maureen, you have a long history in the region. You were born in Michigan and started your career there. If you were advising someone new to the region on ways to build trust there, what would you recommend? A lot of people in our field take local leadership roles in communities where they have zero background.

That happened to me in my past roles in Phoenix and Indianapolis. My advice is to spend a lot of time listening. One thing I learned along the way is that economic development has a different definition, no matter where you are. I'll ask, "What is important to move the community ahead? What do people want?" That varies depending on the place. For example, in Arizona, I quickly found out that local communities were funded by sales taxes, not property taxes. There, they might compete for car dealerships, while we in Detroit compete for car plants.

Likewise, I start my strategic plans by asking the community what economic development means to them. And what don't they want?

Us, too. Before we bring a project or business into a town, we ask if its leaders and residents want it. If they say no, we walk away.

We've seen examples where a business is expanding in a community that doesn't want to grow. I've heard from economic development colleagues in other regions that their lives have been threatened, that they have people following them out of public meetings. We want to avoid that at all costs. The first question we ask when we're considering where a company could locate is "Does the community want it?"

What can be done to mitigate public backlash?

There's a company in Detroit that consults organizations that are doing something big in the community realm, like expanding their business or seeking a local policy change. The company assesses who the supporters are and who the detractors are. Then they'll develop separate communication strategies for both groups. That approach could be helpful everywhere.

I really enjoyed working with y'all on the region's Build Back Better Regional Challenge program's application process. You have such strong professionals on your team at DRP. How do you coach your staff on ways to build trust?

You'll recall that we had a big group of leaders advising the grant application, like seventy or eighty people in every meeting. Each time we met, I would ask them, "Who is not here but needs to be?" Then we would add them to future calls, so the advisory group got bigger along the way.

You're a role model for inclusivity, Maureen. I've also heard themes of transparency and reliability throughout our conversation. What

else do I need to know about your trust-building skills before we wrap up?

I've always been a glass-half-full person. That comes to asking for help or asking for money. If you believe in something strongly enough, then you shouldn't have a problem asking.

I've seen that part of you in action. When Maureen is enthusiastic about something, it's contagious!

We can thank our competitive nature. We believe we can be successful, and it is paying off. Detroit's got its swagger back.

YOUR CALL TO ACTION

I hope the interviews in Part 2 have inspired you to commit to building trust in your own community. You've learned that greater trust is attainable with skills that you already possess. Activating it just requires intentionality. And that heightened trust among local leaders translates into accelerated progress, stronger economies, and confidence to pursue more impactful projects.

This final section shares a summary of the tactics I gathered from Trust Builder interviews that you can use to shape your action plan. By taking these next steps and applying your Trust Strengths, you have the power to curate a culture of trust that helps your community thrive.

37

THE SIX TRUST TACTICS

After the interviews, I took time to reflect on themes that I heard, with you in mind. I discovered that while Trust Builders' communities and experiences differ, their approaches are similar. In fact, it is remarkable how the nature of what they do is consistent whether they live in a rural town or lead a statewide organization, are a private sector volunteer or a government employee. Their lessons are not complex but rather, at least on paper, quite simple. They require intention and courage versus capital.

What specifically can you do to improve local trust, starting tomorrow? I've summarized the themes into six tactics:

1. Show up and follow up.

☐ **Always follow through, and do so in a timely manner.** This is the most consistent advice that Trust Builders shared during my interviews. Do what you say you will do when you're assigned a task. Have a forty-eight-hour rule to send an email acknowledging your next steps, for example. Also, follow up with others in unexpected ways. Small gestures can result in big trust. Remember a personal detail about someone and ask them about it the next time you meet, or send a handwritten note of gratitude.

☐ **Personally attend meetings.** While you can't be everywhere all the time, make sure you attend mission-critical meetings. Practice declining offers, and don't set an expectation that you'll be there if you know you probably won't. Identify high-integrity individuals on your team to serve as proxies, if needed.

☐ **Be a steady influence around others.** Reliability also means that when you show up, you keep a level head. Sporadic personalities can derail meetings and make people wish that person didn't show up at all. You will undoubtedly feel frustrated at times, but take those frustrations out at the gym, in your journal, or with a confidant, not in the middle of a community meeting. Be the stabilizing force.

2. Regularly convene local leaders.

☐ **Establish a cadence for meetings with other local leaders.** Whether there is a pressing issue at hand or you need time to confer and share updates, adhere to the schedule. This creates the safe spaces I described earlier. You might have several regularly scheduled get-togethers. For example, there might be a monthly breakfast with a small group of local leaders, such as your board chair, an elected official, and a college leader. A Friday morning meeting with your staff. A quarterly board meeting and a quarterly gathering with a broader ecosystem of local leaders. Whatever they are, schedule them well in advance and commit to being there.

☐ **Meet to strengthen connections as much as to work on projects.** Keep those meetings on the calendar even when there is no pressing issue. Convening for networking's sake helps form friendships and strengthen bonds. Those connections set a higher baseline for action when more critical matters are at hand. (This might be hard to reconcile in today's fifteen-minute virtual meeting culture, but Trust Builders reinforced that there is nothing more valuable than human contact for building relationships and trust.)

☐ **Always have an agenda and a meeting outcome in mind.** Whether meeting in a concerted way to solve a single issue or to break bread and share stories, ensure there is an agenda and a desired end goal. For the former, the agenda might be as detailed as assigning times and speaking roles, handouts, or even talking points for speakers. For the latter, the agenda could include opening remarks plus a group activity. Whatever it is, know what the "one thing" is that you want the meeting to achieve and build the agenda around that.

☐ **Include time for listening in every meeting.** Give an opportunity for everyone to speak up. In formal meetings, this might include roundtable updates from each participant or a breakout session in which participants can discuss issues in smaller groups. In informal gatherings, consider an icebreaker that connects people one-on-one. Before the meeting, consider the attendees' temperaments. Try to pair more introverted individuals with people who are strong, active listeners and facilitators.

3. Proactively share information.

☐ **Engage in timely and honest conversations.** Do not shy away from sharing bad news, and do so thoughtfully as soon as you can. Use data to support those conversations. Benchmarking your community's performance against others may be helpful. If you hear scuttlebutt around a certain person or initiative, let those people know soon. If doing this is far too uncomfortable for you, ask someone on your team with the Trust Strength of transparency to help you.

☐ **Adopt a "no surprises" mindset.** If something new crops up that could impact a local leader or community group, let them know before that event takes place or the news is made public.

☐ **Schedule regular communications.** Start by understanding

your audiences and the most appropriate communication plat-
forms and timing for each one. Identify an appropriate cadence
for conveying information based on their preferences. A quarterly in-person update might work for one group, when a brief
Monday morning email update might be best for another.

☐ **Use consistent vocabulary.** Using the same words in every
interaction helps frame the information you're sharing. "This
news," for example, "relates to our goal of _________________,
and that goal has been the same for the past five years." A
shared lexicon provides context and confidence in the information you're sharing. You could even count it as a win when
others in the community begin to use the same vocabulary.

4. Find common ground.

☐ **Start with "could we all agree that…"** I've heard various
ways of describing this: finding the center of the Venn diagram
or the least common denominator. What is one thing, no matter
how basic, that local stakeholders can agree on? Can you reflect
on history and say, "This isn't a new issue for us. Although it
feels intense right now, there is no one person to blame." It
might start with a shared desire for the community to have
quality jobs and higher-level incomes, or for the community to
retain families, have a stronger tax base to maintain public
services, or improve education offerings. Whatever it is, find the
one thing that everyone can agree on and start there. State it out
loud.

☐ **Develop and communicate a shared community vision and
goals.** Strategic planning processes that involve a broad range of
stakeholders can be a way to find closer alignment. This is my
area of expertise, and I have seen firsthand how impactful a
community-wide strategy can be. That said, it also requires
successfully executing the plan, which works when multiple
local leaders repeat the agreed-upon vision and goal statements
across diverse audiences over time.

☐ **Recognize that systems and structures can either support or**

discourage trust. Perhaps the one thing local leaders can agree on is that the city council's structure creates neighborhood divisiveness or that the required process for constructing a new building is overly cumbersome, causing a rift between local government and developers. Whatever it is, it can be helpful to recognize that the structure itself is causing trust problems and not the people themselves. If local leaders all agree that the core challenge is the system, not each other, that lays the groundwork for greater collaboration.

5. Give others the spotlight.

☐ **Readily share credit with others.** For some, this can be a tough tactic to implement. I've observed and heard from Trust Builders that there are many times when a group of local leaders works endless hours to bring a project to fruition, only to have a person who was relatively uninvolved take center stage at the ribbon-cutting (governors or mayors, for example; no disrespect intended). That is the nature of the role of being a local leader. Find other ways to celebrate and reward team players outside of the podium moment.

☐ **Celebrate other local leaders' wins.** Go out there and cheer when other local leaders achieve a milestone moment. Being there for them, even if it's a win that you may not have originally supported, goes a long way to building trust. Show up to their event and tout their accomplishments when you talk with others.

☐ **Build humility into organizational values.** Especially for younger professionals, giving others credit for their work can be frustrating. Consider incorporating that into your organization's values or purpose statements. "We strive to support our city's prosperity and celebrate others when progress is made." (Or whatever statement is helpful.) Putting this into words gives your team members a touchstone for recognizing their contributions, even when the recognition is given during a staff or board meeting rather than a public groundbreaking.

6. Focus on long-term outcomes.

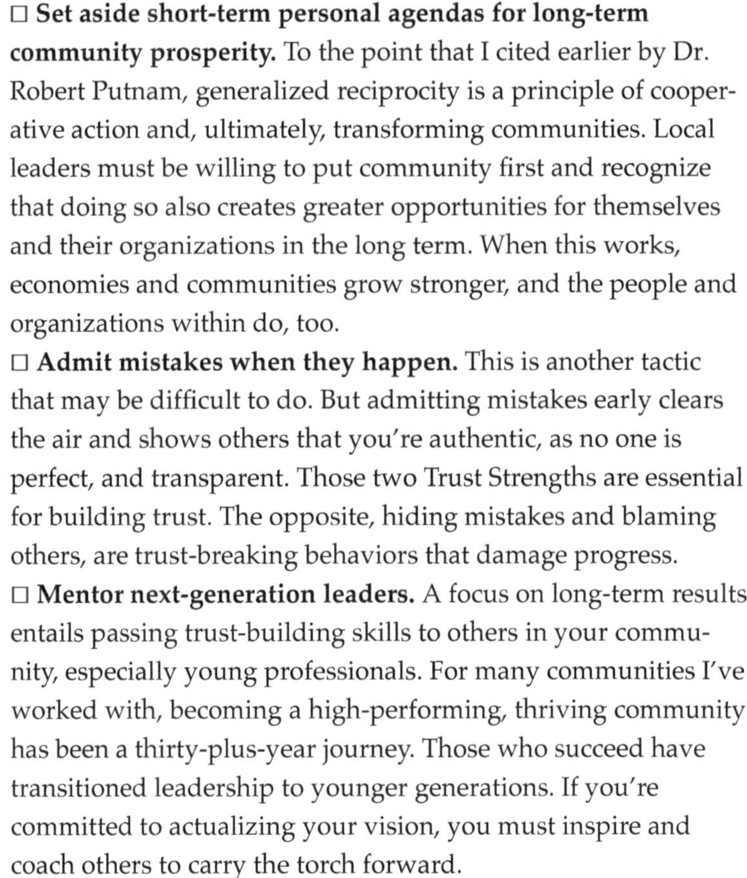

☐ **Set aside short-term personal agendas for long-term community prosperity.** To the point that I cited earlier by Dr. Robert Putnam, generalized reciprocity is a principle of cooperative action and, ultimately, transforming communities. Local leaders must be willing to put community first and recognize that doing so also creates greater opportunities for themselves and their organizations in the long term. When this works, economies and communities grow stronger, and the people and organizations within do, too.

☐ **Admit mistakes when they happen.** This is another tactic that may be difficult to do. But admitting mistakes early clears the air and shows others that you're authentic, as no one is perfect, and transparent. Those two Trust Strengths are essential for building trust. The opposite, hiding mistakes and blaming others, are trust-breaking behaviors that damage progress.

☐ **Mentor next-generation leaders.** A focus on long-term results entails passing trust-building skills to others in your community, especially young professionals. For many communities I've worked with, becoming a high-performing, thriving community has been a thirty-plus-year journey. Those who succeed have transitioned leadership to younger generations. If you're committed to actualizing your vision, you must inspire and coach others to carry the torch forward.

These tactics are echoed in Chapter 5, the Trust Strengths of Trust Builders, as well as in the transcripts in Part 2. If the above list becomes your playbook, think about how these tactics are at work in your own community today. Ask yourself, *which ones are we doing well? Which ones need improvement? What other essential actions would I add to this list that might be unique to my locale?*

You might even make a copy of this chapter and use the check boxes to help you determine when trust building is genuinely at work in your community. Also, the www.TrustBuildersBook.com website provides a copy of these six tactics for download.

245

38

YOUR CALL TO ACTION

This book began with questions I've contemplated for decades: What if trust were the single most powerful driver of local prosperity? If the answer is "yes, it is," how would that insight change the way places approach economic and community development? Would local leaders rethink how they engage with others in their communities? Prioritize their daily tasks? Invest in their own professional development?

We've learned that what seems like an amorphous topic, building trust for the good of your local community, is actually very attainable. There are daily actions you can take to establish, maintain, and repair trust, and those actions can drive community progress far more than almost any other factor. This book shares specific tactics that you can begin using today. It also helps you recognize the trust-building strengths you already have and provides ideas for putting them to work in your community.

Places with trust-based cultures consistently outperform others in economic growth and community development. Interviews with Trust Builders and my own observations over a thirty-year career reinforce this premise. Yes, places with low trust levels will continue to win projects and see growth. A lot of forces are at play, of course, including sheer luck. But those cities and regions that experience sustained, long-term growth and are highly resilient when faced with crises have strong foundations of trust among local leaders.

I also can't overstate the importance of optimism. The communities that thrive are the ones that choose to believe in what's possible. The Trust Builders I interviewed are optimistic people. When leaders choose positivity over cynicism, collaboration usurps competition. I believe positivity grows when one is involved in an opportunity that they feel passionately about.

But passion alone cannot turn a negative thinker into an eternal optimist. Optimism becomes contagious when people experience success together. This book cannot change a person's persona, but it can remind them that mindset goes a long way toward making transformative change in a community.

THANK YOU

Thank you for your curiosity and for taking the time from your busy schedule to learn. I am deeply grateful to you and everyone who informed this book and inspired me throughout my career. I appreciate the more than two hundred places and 20,000+ local community leaders who, over the past thirty years, have shown me that very good things are happening across the country every single day.

I recognize that reading, self-assessing, and reflecting on your own Trust Strengths takes courage and humility. If you've made it to this point in the book, you're already a Trust Builder, and your community is better for it.

Thank you for caring enough to invest time in something bigger than yourself, shaping the future of your community. My hope is that this book gives you confidence and tools to continue trust-building and that your work will lead to even greater prosperity in the place where you live.

YOUR MONDAY MORNING CHALLENGE

Now that you've completed the book, know your Trust Strengths, and feel inspired by the Trust Builder interviews, what's next? I challenge you to start applying what you've learned by taking three steps:

Step one: Identify your top Trust Strength (see table below)

Step two: Pair it with one of the six tactics from the Trust Builder framework (see table below)

Step three: Turn this into a tangible personal commitment: "Starting Monday morning, I will _________________ to establish/reinforce/repair trust in my community." Here are just a few examples of what this could look like:

a. Reliability + Proactively Sharing Information → Commit to distributing a weekly report documenting progress on a specific community project
b. Respecting Differences + Finding Common Ground → Host conversations to find consensus around a community challenge and include people with varied opinions. Create a safe space where those conversations happen on a regular cadence.
c. Active Listening + Giving Others the Spotlight → Meet with another local leader to learn the details of one of their recent wins and then showcase that leader at your next board meeting

Trust Strength	Trust Builder Tactic
Active listening (c.)	Show up and follow up
Authenticity	Regularly convene local leaders
Competency	Proactively share information (a.)
Empathy	Find common ground (b.)
Integrity	Give others the spotlight (c.)
Reliability (a.)	Focus on long-term outcomes
Respecting Differences (b.)	
Transparency	

To solidify your commitment, I encourage you to write it down and add it to your calendar. Speak it into reality during your conversations with others or in presentations.

As you can see, taking action can be easy. Building trust does not need to be a complicated assignment. But imagine if you weren't the only person in the community committed to strengthening trust. What if your team and board members did as well? Your larger ecosystem of local leaders? What if fifty people in your community agreed to do just one thing? A hundred people?

You see my point. If other local leaders adopt this way of thinking, it has the potential to be even more impactful, driving your community from interpersonal and institutional trust toward an entire culture of trust and the positive impacts that follow.

ONGOING COLLABORATION

Think about the collective momentum if every reader of this book took just one trust-building action starting this week. That's how movements start.

I am committed to continuing this research well into the future. This book isn't the finish line; it's an invitation to keep going. Through my consulting firm, Aha! Advisors (www.ah-advisor.com), and my role as Practitioner-in-Residence at Harvard Kennedy School, I will expand upon this to include additional interviews with Trust Builders in places big and small, urban and rural, across America. My ongoing work will include speaking engagements, workshops, writing, research, and strategic planning.

I welcome you to join me on this journey. Scan the QR code on the "Thank You" page that follows to join the Trust Builders network, share your own Trust Builder story, receive updates, access the Trust Strengths assessment, invite me to speak at your next event, host a workshop, or brainstorm about what a trust-based strategic plan could look like for your community.

Together, we can build a national movement of communities that choose trust, lead with optimism, and thrive because of it.

THANK YOU FOR READING MY BOOK!

To contact me, share your story, or access the Trust Strengths assessment,
Scan the QR code:

I appreciate your interest in my book and value your feedback, as it helps me improve future Trust Builder interviews and research. I would appreciate it if you could leave your invaluable review on Amazon.com with your feedback. Thank you!

ABOUT THE AUTHOR

Amy Holloway is a national economic and community development strategist with more than thirty years of experience, having worked with more than 200 U.S. communities. The inclusive planning processes that she facilitates often involve hundreds of stakeholders in a client community. Over the course of her career, she has engaged one-on-one with 20,000 or more local leaders from the private, public, nonprofit, and education sectors.

Amy has served regions like Asheville, Atlanta, Austin, Chattanooga, Charleston, Charlotte, Cincinnati, Cleveland, Columbus, Detroit, Houston, Jacksonville, Miami, Richmond, Sonoma County, and many others. She currently serves as Practitioner-in-Residence at Harvard Kennedy School's Reimaging the Economy Project.

For the first twenty-five years of her career, she lived in Austin, Texas, where she had the privilege of working with community leaders who helped shape Austin's tremendous economic success. She established Avalanche Consulting in 2005 and grew the firm to become a go-to strategist for some of the most dynamic communities in the country.

In 2020, a Big 4 consulting firm acquired Avalanche. As a partner at the firm and leader of its national economic development practice, she continued to work with communities across the country seeking more resilient economies. She supported dozens of communities through the COVID-19-related economic downturn.

In 2024, she retired from the Big 4 partnership and started her newest project: Aha! Her work continues to center on economic and community development strategies and leadership alignment. It is founded on her belief that trust among leaders is the most important contributor to a community's success.

She holds BBS and MS degrees, both in economics, from Baylor University. She resides in Asheville, North Carolina, with her husband and two tenacious terriers.